WALKS TO
YORKSHIRE WATERFALLS

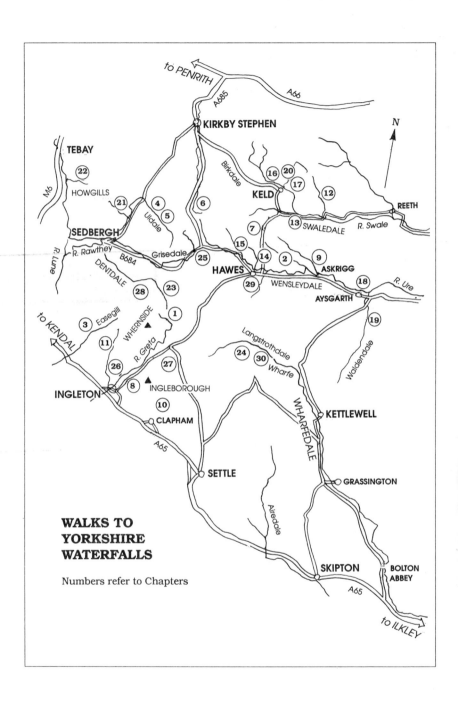

**WALKS TO
YORKSHIRE
WATERFALLS**

Numbers refer to Chapters

WALKS TO
YORKSHIRE WATERFALLS

by
MARY WELSH

Illustrated by
LINDA WATERS

CICERONE PRESS

MILNTHORPE, CUMBRIA

ISBN 1 85284 062 5

'notice the milestones' (page 108)

CONTENTS

1. Force Gill, Whernside...............9
2. Disher Force and Cat Leap Waterfall, Wensleydale.................13
3. Cow Dub, Ease Gill, Barbondale 18
4. Lower Falls, River Rawthey, Uldale..23
5. Lower Falls and Upper Falls, Uldale...27
6. Shaws & Hell Gill Force, Mallerstang 32
7. The Buttertubs, Jenny Whalley Force, Swaledale
   and High Force above Ravenseat, Birk Dale 37
8. White Scar Caves and Ingleborough...43
9. Mill Gill & Whitfield Gill Force, Askrigg, Wensleydale.............49
10. Gaping Gill and the Reginald Farrer Trail, Ingleborough..........55
11. Yordas Cave, Kingsdale..60
12. Gunnerside Gill, Swaledale..63
13. Ellas's Stot Wood & by Muker, Swaledale...............................70
14. Hardraw Force, Wensleydale..75
15. Cotter Force, Wensleydale..78
16. River Swale, west of Keld, Swaledale 82
17. River Swale, east of Keld, Swaledale.......................................85
18. Aysgarth Falls, Wensleydale..89
19. Cauldron Falls, Walden Beck, West Burton,
    Wensleydale...93
20. Wain Wath Force, Swaledale 96
21. Cautley Spout, Howgills...98
22. Black Force, Carlin Gill, Howgills 103
23. Scow Force and Dent Head Viaduct, Dentdale......................108
24. Hagg Beck, Horse Head Moor, Langstrothdale......................111
25. Clough Force between Garsdale & Grisedale 115
26. The Waterfalls Walk, Ingleton...119
27. Alum Pot, Selside, Ribblesdale 127
28. Arten Gill Viaduct & Dockra Bridge, Dentdale 132
29. Aysgill Force, Gayle and Mossdale Viaduct, Wensleydale........136
30. River Wharfe, Langstrothdale 140

5

Halton Gill - 'the church and the school are private dwellings' (page 113)

FOREWORD

In this book I take readers to some of the lovely, remote corners of a delightful part of northern England. In each chapter I describe the route to the waterfall and, depending on the season, the birds, flowers and animals that might be seen. My intention is that readers will experience the pleasure of seeing a yellow hammer or redstart in the same location as I did, year after year.

I hope readers' hearts will lift, as mine has done, as they pass through the Dales in their quest for more waterfalls and the peace of the countryside enfolds them. I hope, like me, they will revel in the feeling of timelessness as they see the ancient walls about the well stocked pastures and the sturdy barns in good repair.

And I hope that as they stride across the high moors, or descend into caves in search of dancing waterfalls they will feel, as I feel, that this part of the north is heaven indeed.

For all the walks I recommend walking boots and good waterproofs. Take the relevant O.S. map - the Outdoor Leisure series for the Dales at 1:25,000 is advisable. Take plenty of food and drink, especially when the waterfall is several miles over wild moorland.

My thanks go to all those who have encouraged me to seek out the hidden corners of Yorkshire; to Linda Waters, who has illustrated the walks with such a sure and sympathetic touch and to my family and friends who have walked, so patiently, with me. Lastly I must not fail to mention my border collie, Cammie, who has accompanied me on all my happy wanderings.

Force Gill

1. Force Gill, Whernside

MR 758820 - 755823, 6 miles

A T INGLETON take the B6255 in the direction of Hawes. The
houses of the Yorkshire town are soon left behind and rolling
green pastures with criss-crossing limestone walls and the leafless
trees of January delight the eye. After five and a half miles the
Batty Moss Viaduct curves away to the left with Whernside beyond
- the top of the peak, with snow streaking its gullies, lost in mist.
Pass under the railway line and park in the lay-by on the right just
beyond the B6479. The path to the waterfalls leads off in the
direction of the viaduct opposite the lay-by and is signposted
Whernside.

The path comes to the base of the 23 soaring pillars that support
the viaduct. Every fifth one is robustly buttressed but those
between are slender and elegant, and several are under repair.
Continue along the path that passes elder bushes now in leaf. A
crow sits on a post and 'pawks' mournfully. Climb the stile ahead
and walk on along a very wet area to the start of a reinforced track.
This runs beside the railway line and has been built by using a
plastic mesh carpet covered with four to five inches of slate
chippings. This track continues as far as Bleamoor sidings,
carrying the walker over a quagmire of mud and moor, a deterrent
to straying and adding to the erosion. It ends in a sea of mud.

Walk on, keeping close to the wall of a derelict house, once the
home of the signalman. This area, very wet for a few yards, soon
improves. Do not be tempted to move away from the wall and onto
the moor, which is an extensive area of marsh. Follow the path to
the edge of the Little Dale Beck, crossing by convenient boulders,
and then bear to the left. Here the railway line descends into the
black maw of Bleamoor Tunnel. Rabbits preen and doze on the
steep slopes of the cutting. The walled path runs across a bridge
high over the line and beside the path is the aqueduct that diverts
the Force Gill Beck well away from the track. The aqueduct is

The aqueduct that diverts Force Gill beck

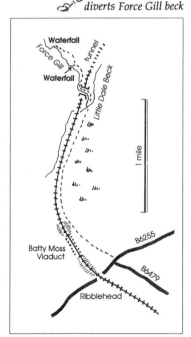

sturdily constructed and well designed for its job. The pretty common spleenwort grows in the crevices of the stonework. Pass through the gate and walk up the reinforced path. To the left of the track lies the first spectacular fall. To reach it turn left before the gate and walk along an indistinct path to a grassy eminence overlooking the splendid waterfall.

The beck drops precipitously over a lip of rock in the centre of an amphitheatre of gritstone. First it cascades over shallow steps and then the wind catches the water and pulls it into the air before it descends in a curtain of water. Behind this curtain small streams form tiny falls as they bounce off ledges too narrow to impede the main flow. Spray, and the noise of falling water, fill the hollow. A raven flies slowly overhead and then is lost in the low cloud over Whernside. Rowan, birch and heather grow around the rim of the semicircle of rock.

Return half-way along the path and then strike up the hillside, where the pretty cladonia lichen is

10

bright red among the bleached grass, to a higher path that runs along the top of the precipice. This gives another grand view of Force Beck flowing sedately to the lip before descending with such magnificence. Walk on along the beck to the next fall, a wide shallow step of rock over which the beck surges white and fast into several boiling pools. Continue beside the mountain stream using sheep trods for easy access to the next fall. Here the Force races across rock pavement before swirling round huge squat boulders to rage in white tresses into a foaming basin.

Follow the trods until ahead lies a fairyland of waterfalls. Force Beck, so aptly named, descends a dozen or more rock steps in a series of sparkling, gurgling falls. Pause here and wonder at the vista ahead before crossing a tributary and a track to Whernside. Continue scrambling into this picturesque gill, where mountain hares teased the writer's dog. Turn right when at first it seems the head of the gill is reached. Once round the sharpish corner a spectacular fall lies ahead. The beck plummets over a ledge, high up on a precipitous ridge, falling in a long white foaming plume of water and spray is picked up by the wind - a splendid climax to an exciting walk.

Force Gill -
a spectacular fall

11

Cat Leap Waterfall

Force and Cat Leap Waterfall, near Askrigg, Wensleydale

MR 981904 - 960909, 6 mile

O N A balmy day in mid-January the sun frequently breaks through the few remaining clouds that brought the night's rain - rain that filled the becks and increased the tempestuousness of the falls. In spite of this mildness, the distant fell tops still seem less alluring than the rolling pastures about Askrigg, the chief town of Upper Wensleydale. It is from this solid, compact town that the walk to the two waterfalls begins.

Park in front of St Oswald's Church, often called the 'Cathedral of Wensleydale.' Walk up the main street, lined with tightly packed houses, past the King's Arms Hotel and the Crown Inn. Just beyond the left turn to Oxnop and Muker look for a signposted stile on the left side of the road giving the direction for Newbiggin. Climb uphill, passing through several gated stiles, and then turn right behind a cottage to another stile. From here strike diagonally uphill, passing through several well-maintained gap stiles. These stiles provide excellent access, though their narrowness, intended

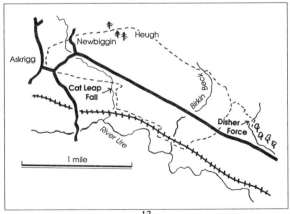

to prevent stock from passing through, could cause problems for the well built fell wanderer.

After climbing the last stile the walker enters a farm track. Here turn right. Look for the pretty falls to the left of the track, beneath ash and alder. Walk on a few yards to the tiny green surrounded by the brown stone houses of Newbiggin. Follow the direction given by the footpath sign. After passing through a gate bear left, crossing the pastures in a diagonal direction, walking steadily uphill through walled pastures. Each stile is waymarked in yellow and these guiding marks continue on the walls of a cluster of farm buildings.

Pass through the gate beyond and walk up the path leading through an extensive area of larch and beech where blue tits chatter cheerily. Walk through the gap in the wall on the right and continue in a diagonal direction to a stile onto Heugh Lane. Turn

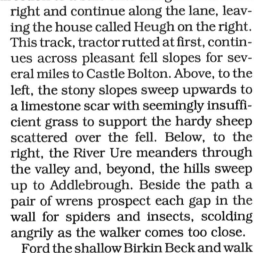

right and continue along the lane, leaving the house called Heugh on the right. This track, tractor rutted at first, continues across pleasant fell slopes for several miles to Castle Bolton. Above, to the left, the stony slopes sweep upwards to a limestone scar with seemingly insufficient grass to support the hardy sheep scattered over the fell. Below, to the right, the River Ure meanders through the valley and, beyond, the hills sweep up to Addlebrough. Beside the path a pair of wrens prospect each gap in the wall for spiders and insects, scolding angrily as the walker comes too close.

Ford the shallow Birkin Beck and walk on, following the track as it drops downhill towards Woodhall. Here, where the cart track leads down to the village, pass through a gate on the left

'close by the pool - ivy'

and turn right, continuing along the route towards Castle Bolton. The walled track, muddy in winter, leads to another ford. Pass through the gate beyond the racing stream and then turn right, climbing down steep stepped rocks to a path along the edge of a ravine. From this path there is a good view of the lovely Disher Force.

The beck leaps over a gap in the limestone, tumbling white-topped over a ledge, into a deep pool. It continues its wild descent in foam-

'tumbling over ledge after ledge'

ing cascades into a dark hollow before it starts its placid journey on its way to join the Ure. The ravine is lined with ash and sycamore and close by the pool grow holly and ivy with large glossy leaves. Look for the rusty machinery beside the Force that once provided electricity for the houses in the valley.

Return along the walled track to the gate and take the farm track that leads down to the cluster of buildings on either side of the road from Askrigg to Castle Bolton. Here cross over

'continues in foaming cascades'

15

and walk down the lane signposted Woodhall. Enjoy this sheltered lane, where spring seems very close. Look for the steamroller and the gypsy caravan on the left and the huge clumps of snowdrops in the cottage gardens. Pass through the farm and continue down the lane to the old railway track, and turn right along the footpath on the far side following the yellow waymark signs again.

Just beyond the beck that flows through Birkin Gill (forded earlier on the walk) pass through a metal gate onto the dismantled railway. This is a lovely part of the walk with gently sloping grassy banks edging the greensward track. Here a flock of redwings settle in an ash and then fly off towards berried hawthorns. A large bend in the River Ure brings the surging water close to the edge of the track.

Follow the waymarks that direct the walker to the right of the track. Walk on to the wall ahead and turn right walking uphill to a stile in the wall. Overhead flies a heron on its way, perhaps, to feed in the Ure. Pass through and continue to the edge of the beck. Walk upstream to Cat Leap, a glorious waterfall hidden deep in a grotto-like ravine. The beck elegantly descends under sycamores into a narrow cleft, then foams furiously at its imprisonment. Its passage is guarded by a huge clump of polypody fern with large bright green fronds. On the beck's further bank grow primroses cradled by their crinkled blue-green leaves and dense mats of moss.

Walk uphill away from the fall, keeping beside the wall, to a stile - the most awkward of the walk, seemingly designed for very long-legged Yorkshiremen. Turn left and walk diagonally across the pasture to another stile. Cross the beck on convenient stones and walk up the slope to the stile in the wall across the pasture. From here the path passes through a series of stiles to the road just on the edge of Askrigg.

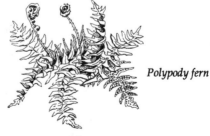

Polypody fern

Cow Dub

3. Cow Dub, Ease Gill, Barbondale

MR 675805, 3¹/₂ miles

TAKE THE A683 Kirby Lonsdale to Sedbergh road and turn right just before the Casterton village name plate signposted High Casterton. Continue along this road until signposted cross-roads are reached. The road to Bullpot straight on (Cowan Bridge and Settle), is narrow with few passing places. At the next junction turn right, then immediately left on an unsigned road. After a short distance it climbs rapidly through a beech wood and then continues up and up onto the open fell. Here a kestrel hovers low over the bleached grass, methodically seeking prey by dropping downwards every few seconds or so. A flock of green plover, black and white in the misty February sky, wheel and dive.

The lonely road, after coming very close to the edge of the steep

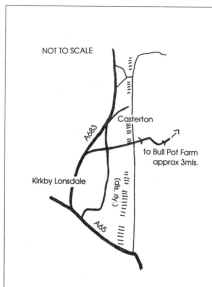

slopes down to the Leck, drops downhill to Bullpot Farm, now used as a pot-holing centre. Park on the grassy verge at the end of the tarmacked road and before the farm. Pass through the gate at the far side of the farm to the start of the track to the waterfall. The gate is dedicated to a pot-holer who lost his life in 1980. A paving slab lies across a little beck and snowdrops grow in profusion. The buds on the ash that crowd the farm are big and black.

Follow the stony track out on to Casterton Fell, past the Bullpot of the Witches on the

18

right. This pot-hole lies beneath many ash trees and the little beck, just crossed, drops noisily into its depths. Just beyond, to the left of the path, another pot-hole drops away into inky darkness. Take care when looking into these seemingly bottomless but fascinating pits.

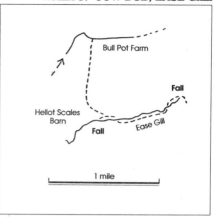

Further along the path look for the crumbling limekilns. Continue along the track beside the fell wall to a gate and stile, ahead. Here black, twisted droppings reveal the presence of a fox.

Walk on along the narrower path, straight ahead, beyond the gate. It continues over the bleak moorland to the ruins of Hellot Scales Barn. The path comes to the edge of a deep depression in which lies the dry bed of the river. Bird song fills the air, in great contrast to the silent moor. A flock of fieldfares utter low warbling refrains before flying off to trees further down the valley. As they go they call harshly and display their whitish undersides. A blackbird gives its loud alarm call and a robin ticks fiercely from a thorn bush.

'snowdrops'

Turn left and walk down the steepish path into the hollow and cross over to the wire mesh fence. Climb over, where others have climbed before, and move carefully to the edge of a moss-covered limestone outcrop. Below lies Ease Gill Kirk with its dry waterfall of white limestone, free of moss. Overhead grow sycamores with fat green buds and holly and ivy with glossy, dark green leaves.

19

Ease Gill above the waterfall

This secret hollow, bordered with ferns, is the haunt of blue tits, chaffinches and a single mistle thrush that sings unconcerned by human intruders from the highest branch of the tallest tree.

Return to the indistinct path beyond the fence and follow it to the edge of the dry river bed above the dry fall and cross to the other bank. Continue along the path as it moves deep into Ease Gill. The path beside the dry river bed, grassy for most of the way, passes below high limestone outcrops. Large ash trees grow out from cracks between the rock layers, their roots lost behind the limestone. Honeysuckle clambering over what it can is in leaf. Polypody and spleenwort flourish among the boulders and silver birch trees have tiny soft catkins. Five ravens, with slow measured flight, pass overhead croaking gutturally as they go. Sheep graze on the higher slopes.

Look for the pot-holes along the side of the path at the base of the limestone outcrops. Listen for the sound of rushing water behind the rocks, hidden waterfalls the noise of which contrasts strangely with the dry beck. Higher into the gill the slopes becomes steeper and crowd in on the gill bottom. At this point cross the rocky bed to the grassy flats on the other side, avoiding some awkward scrambling. Ahead the gill seems blocked by a barrier of limestone, but as you approach you can see that a great cleft splits the rock wall. From this huge incision comes the sound of tumbling water. Walk ahead carefully into the shadow of the fissure. Awesome wet blocks of stone almost touch overhead. Immediately ahead water drops many feet into a basin high above the walker's head. Another long, foaming jet leaps from this pool and plummets down into a smooth-edged, kidney-shaped pool. The rim is wet and covered with slippery tuffa and care is again needed. Close to your feet the clear water lies several feet deep. Under the waterfall itself the water is dark and seemingly very deep indeed. Now it becomes clear why the beck is dry. The water is lost underground.

High above this narrow canyon, filled with the sound of falling water, grow rowans and a mass of fern. Look for the huge pot-hole to the left of the waterfall. Climb up beside the cavern. Above the deep cleft the beck races along a water slide. Above this the beck can be seen flowing sedately through the rock-strewn Ease Gill. Find a limestone platform a little way from the great cleft. Here you can picnic in the February sunlight out of the wind.

'A robin ticks fiercely from a thorn bush'

Uldale - Lower Falls

4. Lower Falls on the River Rawthey, Uldale

MR 728967, 3¹/₂ miles

E ARLY MARCH brings pastures full of lambs, twins with white curly wool and twins with black faces, feet and tails. Leafless woodland trees shelter a carpet of pale lemon daffodils that have replaced the earlier white drift of snowdrops. Birds sit together, or fly close, busy with their nests or the responsibilities of incubation.

On the fell winter holds sway - small pools topped with ice, grass bleached and limp, buds on gnarled thorns tightly closed and summer migrants still absent.

Park in the large space on the left-hand side of the road just before the Rawthey Bridge. The bridge spans the Rawthey 5¹/₂ miles along the A683 road to Kirkby Stephen from Sedbergh. Overhead a buzzard wings slowly and then tries to sit at the top of a small bush. It fails to balance and after blundering through the twigs in another

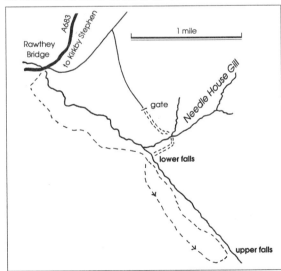

unsuccessful attempt moves off and flies into a small conifer plantation beside the river.

Cross the road and follow the signpost directions for Uldale. Stride over the deeply rutted track into the valley. The air is crisp and cold to one's face. The river, below and

Uldale - 'pasture full of lambs'

away to the left, winds beneath its enfolding ashes and alders. The fells ahead are enticing. All this makes for an exhilarating walk. Keep to the track that swings to the right, skirting a deep, wide moorland pool. Here a heron feeds quietly and flies off only when the writer's dog draws a little too close. Where the track divides,

'a moorland pool'

continue along the left-hand fork keeping parallel with the beck. At times the way crosses small marshy areas that must be circumvented with care. After two miles or so the track drops down to the wide footbridge that crosses the pretty river and provides an excellent platform for viewing the Lower Falls below.

The beck flows quietly, then falls in elegant cascades, foaming white-topped as it rushes

24

Uldale - 'a heron flies off'

through narrow gaps between layers of limestone. At times the hurrying water must flow over these layers but today, after a week of cold, dry weather, its fury and energy is restrained to these gaps. Ash, alder and hazel shadow the water. Below the bridge the beck enters a small canyon. High up grow Scots pine, oak and hazel sheltering the Falls from the icy winds that sweep off the wintry fell. In the canyon flat sheets of limestone are covered with ice and icicles have formed beneath the overhang of the steep sides where the beck has cut away the rock at its base. Bright green ferns and moss have a dusting of snow.

Cross the bridge and walk up the wide track through beech and oak whose rust-coloured leaves hide the soft ground beneath. To the right busy rooks refurbish their nests and there is much traffic to and from the fields and the rookery. Turn left at the end of the track and continue along the farm road, past the verdant Needle House Gill until the gate to the road is reached. Pass through the gate and walk along the narrow road that winds across the moorland. After a mile and a half turn left at the junction and walk downhill to the Rawthey Bridge and the car park.

Uldale Upper Falls

5. Lower Falls and Upper Falls, Uldale

*MR 745946, Rawthey Bridge to Upper Falls return 6¹/₂ miles,
Lower Falls to Upper Falls return 2 miles. (see map p23)*

I N EARLY April drifts of wood anemone patchwork the grassy verges of the Yorkshire roads. Coltsfoot flowers, their golden heads unobscured by the large green leaves yet to come. The hawthorn bushes of the hedgerows carry tiny green leaves and blackthorn is laden with blossom.

Park and walk to the Lower Falls as detailed in Walk 4, or drive over the Rawthey Bridge and follow the signpost directions for Uldale. The turn for this lonely valley bears off to the right immediately beyond the balustrade of the bridge. A mile along the road take the first right turn that leads over the moor and park at the gated end of the road. Pass through the gate and walk on along a farm road, through Needle House Gill, and up the slope beyond.

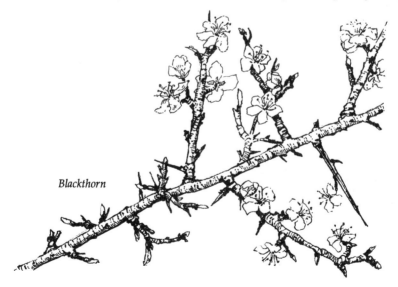

Blackthorn

'Holly - laden with berries'

Turn right through a gate and walk down the steep track, below majestic beeches, to the bridge over the Lower Falls.

Cross the bridge and turn left, following a narrow track along the side of the beck. The air resounds with the songs of meadow pipits. From over the fell come the bubbling calls of curlews, and then the birds fly overhead. Continue along the rock-strewn path as it climbs above the river into the secluded valley. Look down for the first sighting of a lovely waterfall that descends over stepped rocks in a cloud of spray beneath birch, hazel, Scots pine and holly loaded with berries. Walk on into the dale to the next fall where the Rawthey cascades in white foam into a deep basin, this time with no trees to hide its glory.

The narrow path continues at the base of a scree slope. Look for the path as it ascends a steep grassy slope and follow it as it passes more scree and some derelict farm buildings. By taking this track the walker avoids the difficult terrain close by the racing water. A few steps further on, and on the other side of the beck, lies a dramatic fall where a feeder stream drops sharply downwards, the water hurtling pell-mell over steep ledges through a narrow tree-lined gill. A long-tailed kestrel eludes several mobbing rooks when it comes too close to their rookery, then glides away.

Walk on along the path. In the distance lie the Upper Falls, sparkling in the sunshine. Follow the path as it swings up the fellside. Pause by a clump of ash and look down at another lovely fall far below in the sheer-sided gill. Here the water-droplets sparkle, crystal-like, in the bright sun. Proceed with much care along the narrow path as it continues close to the edge of the ravine. The elegant Upper Falls lie ahead. The Rawthey bounces gleefully down several small limestone steps and then drops in long white tresses for twenty feet or more into a foaming pool. From here it cascades over more ridges of rock until it hurries on through the ravine. Rowan and ash cover the steep slopes and the many larch that grow here are covered with tiny soft-green needles. Spend time enjoying this glorious fall.

Climb the slopes above to a path that traverses the top of the fell. Turn right. Ahead lie the Howgills, bathed in sunlight, with fleeting shadows sliding over the slopes as a cloud passes. Walk along this delightful high level track, which gives the walker a bird's-eye view

'a feeder stream drops sharply downwards'

of Yorkshire. Small farms scatter the lower slopes, each with its sheltering trees. Drystone walls criss-cross the pastures and sturdy stone barns dot the fields.

Continue along the narrow path, following it as it drops down to the bridge over the Lower Falls. The walker can then return over the moorland track to the Rawthey Bridge or climb the wide path through the trees, turning left at the gate and following the farm track to the gate at the road end.

Hell Gill

6. Shaws & Hell Gill Force, Mallerstang

MR 796948 - 779966, 4 miles

LEAVE SEDBERGH or Hawes by the A684 and at the Moorcock Inn take the B6259. Two miles along the road look for a small plantation of conifers on the right. Park on the wide verge opposite a gated track. Walk down the track through the young conifers, where in April the first willow warblers have arrived and a pair of swallows glide overhead. Pass through the gate across the track and continue downhill to the narrow bridge across the hurrying beck. Follow the signpost directions into the large churchyard surrounding the diminutive Lunds church. Sheep and lambs graze the pastures among the gravestones. Some of these have fallen and are blanketed with lichen, other stand proud and it is just possible to read the date on some - 1829 being the earliest found. A heron flies low overhead.

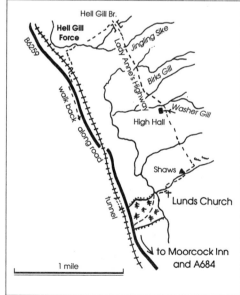

Leave this quiet corner by a small wooden gate in the wall. This leads to a clapper bridge across the beck. Curlews call and give their bubbling call from the fell slopes. Continue beside the beck to another gated gap in the next wall. This gives access to a path in front of an ancient farmhouse. Pass through another gap beyond the farm and climb up to a plank bridge. Yet another gated gap lies ahead. Beyond this climb

32

the steep slope that leads to Shaws, the former youth hostel. To the left, below the house, is a wide grassy way that bridges the beck. Stand on this and look up to see the mountain stream tumbling down the steep slope in a series of tiny stepped falls. The banks are full of primroses, wood anemones and golden saxifrage, and overhead ash, sycamore and rowan are in fat bud. Pause and enjoy this idyllic scene.

Cross a narrow plank bridge by Shaws, pausing as you go to enjoy the splendid waterfall above. The beck races past a drystone wall and drops down in elegant tresses into a tree-lined hollow. Above can be seen two more falls and here the water, caught by the breeze, is dragged into the air. Climb the steep, moss-covered

'the mountain stream tumbling down'

steps out of the hollow to the foot of these higher falls. Look up at the tumbling water racing through a very narrow, sheer-sided gill. Climb beside the beck to the limestone ridge above.

Strike left across the pasture to stone throughs and a ladder stile in the corner. Then walk north along the wide and sometimes muddy track that lies behind the wall - Lady Anne's Highway,

33

named after the 17th century Lady Anne Clifford who inherited the castles of Appleby, Brough, Brougham, Skipton and Pendragon. After repairing and rebuilding the castles she spent the latter part of her life visiting them and caring for the needs of her tenants using the highway on her journeyings.

Ahead and to the far left lies Wild Boar Fell, where sunlight and shade continually alternate as clouds scurry across the sun. To the right of the track the fells slope upwards and from these rise skylarks on quivering wings. They ascend, singing their liquid songs, until they are only specks in the sky and then the trilling ceases as they drop like stones to the pasture below.

Continue along the track, which continues close to a wall where meadow pipits and pied wagtails disport. Walk on past the ruins of High Hall, which stands beside Washer Gill. Cross the beck on convenient stones and take the lower path. This crosses the infant River Ure and then sweeps down towards Hell Gill. Two green

'the diminutive Lunds Church'

plovers wheel and dive over the pastures, courting. Follow the track to Hell Gill Bridge and peer over the parapet to the awesome canyon below through which the beck races. Pass through the gate across the track and the gate to the left. Walk downhill, keeping close to the wall on the left, until a farm lies close by. Here the gill widens and the beck descends in a series of pretty cascades falling into a deep, brown surging pool.

'the banks are full of primroses'

Walk downhill past the farm. A redshank, greyish-brown, red-legged and billed, feeds in the marshy ground. It flies off, showing the black and white markings on its wings, filling the air with its lovely plaintive call. Continue along the track until the railway line lies ahead. Leave the path and strike to the right across the pasture to the edge of the beck and follow it down to where it makes a magnificent descent over the edge of the amphitheatre of limestone rocks - Hell Gill Force. At the top of the forty foot drop the water falls like a fringe over a small ridge before cascading in brilliant white over more shallow ledges. Then, after this gentle start, it falls with great turbulence into a peat-stained basin far below. Celandines, primroses and saxifrage grow at its foot and ash, hawthorn and rowan grow sparsely on its sheer sides. Above

'a redshank ....feeds in the marshy ground'

this lovely force stands a row of ash and beech. About its top a pair of dippers hunt for insects and then fly upstream to feed in the fast-flowing water.

Continue along the track to the road. Turn left and walk the one and a half miles to the start.

35

Buttertubs
36

7. The Buttertubs, Jenny Whalley Force, Swaledale and High Force above Ravenseat, Birk Dale

MR 874962, 863025, 3 miles

IN LATE APRIL blackthorn, laden with blossom, lines the road approaching Hawes. Cowslips flower on grassy banks and a pair of swallows perch close on wires leading to every farmhouse. The gritstone houses, bathed in sunshine, exude a warm welcome to people visiting this small market town which sits at the head of Wensleydale.

From Hawes take Burnt Acres Road for a mile and turn right at the junction in the direction of Hardraw. After a quarter of a mile turn right for Muker and begin the long climb through Buttertubs Pass. Enjoy the extensive views stretching away on either side. Snow still lingers in hollows on the hills. Pale grey walls criss-cross green pastures and barns sit squarely in nearly every field.

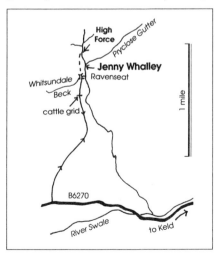

A hundred yards beyond the summit look for a fenced area on the left and a restored stone wall on the right, and park on the wide verge close by. Cross the road and descend the concrete steps that lead to the rim of the deep pot-hole. On the far side of the huge hole a beck hurtles downwards, spraying and fuming in long streamers of sparkling water, falling forty or fifty feet into the darkness. Nearer to the walker, rearing up from the depths, stand the Buttertubs, tall stacks of rock like elephant legs, pale grey and ridged. The stacks have been left free-standing as the rock between has been worn away by water and acidic erosion. The tops of the stacks, worn smooth perhaps by many visitors, stand level with the rim and between each, on ledges and in crevices, thrive a multitude of plants. Flourishing in the moisture-laden, sheltered, lime-rich environment are wood anemone, wood sorrel, wild strawberry, cranesbill, golden saxifrage, hard fern and spleenwort. A rowan clings to the rim, the pink scales of its buds no longer able to restrain the pale green leaves.

Cross the road and view the second pot-hole. Here, too, a small stream - which must become a torrent after rain - drops many feet into a dark hole. More stacks guard the fall and shelter myriads of plants thriving in crevices and in the continual spray. View the depths with care. Another group of stacks lies a few yards down the road and here several rowans grow, sheltered by the pot-hole rim from the icy winds that blow over the pass in the winter.

Above the Buttertubs the slopes stretch upwards to Great Shunner Fell and from here come the lovely spring songs of meadow pipits busy with their nuptials. A black-headed gull with brown head, red bill and legs wings over the pass.

'cowslips'

Why are they called Buttertubs? Some say because farmers on their way home from market stored their unsold butter in the cool recesses of the pot-holes. Others that the name is from the old English word *byden* meaning valley.

Continue down the pass and turn right in the direction of Muker, a small village on the River Swale. Look for the Literary Institute sitting proudly at the centre of the village. Beyond lies the church of St. Mary the Virgin, which once was thatched with heather. After enjoying the hospitality of

The Literary Institute

Muker return along the B6270 by way of Thwaites, Keld and Wain Wath Force (see Walk 20). Cross Hoggarths Bridge and climb the hill. Beyond the cattle-grid at the top look for a parking space on the right at the end of the narrow road to Ravenseat.

The metalled unfenced road swings uphill and moorland lies all around. Curlews fly overhead calling and bubbling to each other as they go. They rise heavily from moorland tufts and fly with strong, measured wing-beats and flashes of white rumps. As they return to their nests their legs dangle, disproportionately long and seemingly unsuitable for an elegant landing. Green plovers, black and white aerial acrobats, utter their haunting musical whistle as they enjoy riding the air currents, then drop lightly and run forward along the ground with crest erect.

Walk on past Hill Top, where a pair of wheatears busily prospect cracks in walls and rocks. Follow the road as it begins to drop downhill into the quiet isolation of Ravenseat. Here, on better pasture, Swaledale sheep, renowned for their hardiness, nurture

Jenny Whalley Force - 'charming cascades'

their white woolly, black-faced lambs. The ewes come forward expecting to be fed, and the lambs, now strong and venturesome, race across the road and gambol over tufts and hillocks. When momentarily losing their nerve, they race back to the comfort and reassurance of the ewe. The wool of the Swaledales, now tangled and matted, will, when shorn, be used for woollens and carpets.

Cross the Whitsundale Beck by the narrow bridge, which possibly dates from the eighteenth century and has recently been restored by the National Park. Walk straight ahead and pass through two farm gates out onto a less muddy track that stays close to Hodds Bottom Beck, where, over a series of rock steps, the beck drops in a flurry of white water. This is Jenny Whalley Force. The water, foam topped, descends in charming cascades to be absorbed into a rich brown pool in the bottom of a small ravine. Here rabbits play among foxgloves, saxifrage, heather and bilberry, and a pair of sandpipers take flight and move upstream.

Continue beside the beck to a ford. Beyond this lies the path through Pryclose Gutter to Tan Hill. From here three dunlins rise and with quiet calls fly fast and direct over the pastures, then are lost to sight as they settle among the tufts of the grass. Do not cross the ford but walk upstream to where the pretty beck - given the grand name of High Force - descends over wide, shallow steps of rock. It drops in elegant cascades in a secluded moorland setting with quietness all around. Here, too, the sandpipers seen earlier stand and bob on rocks about the tumbling waters.

Return along the beck-side path and the road, following the route supposedly taken by the hauliers of Lady Anne Clifford's coal. This was carried from the Tan Hill coal seams to her castle at Pendragon (see Walk 6).

White Scar Caves -
'the noise of falling water fills the air'

8. White Scar Caves and Ingleborough

MR 713746 White Scar Caves, 745746 Ingleborough, 5 miles

L EAVE INGLETON by the B6255 and drive for a mile and a half
in a north-easterly direction. The entrance to the caves lies on
the right-hand side of the road and there is a large car park in front
of the site. Wear jackets or woollies for the tour because the
temperature underground remains at a steady 5 degrees Celsius.
Damp passages, lit by electric light, form the caves. In some places
the roof swells upwards, cathedral-like, and in other is so low you
will have to crouch a little, but nowhere will you feel claustrophobic.

A long passage leads from the entrance into the heart of White
Scar, passing an illuminated cranny with a model representing
Christopher Long who discovered the caves in 1923. The model,
wearing a bowler hat with four candles in its brim, reminds the
visitor of the difficulties with which these early cave explorers had
to cope. The passageway comes to an abrupt end at the foot of the
first waterfall. Crystal-clear water tumbles down its rock-strewn
bed before descending in long white streamers into a continually

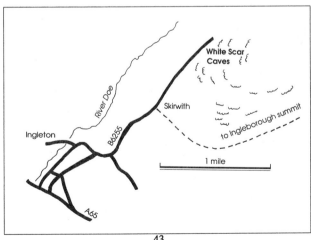

agitated basin. The noise of the falling water fills the air, the walls magnifying the sound. Long had to climb this waterfall before he could continue his explorations. Today the visitor follows a diversion that leads to the top of the fall. Beyond, you will have to crouch a little while walking by a bubbling underground stream.

'swallows ..

The second waterfall lies at the end of this low part, with water dropping many feet in long strands of sparkling droplets. Sometimes after heavy rain the visitor has to move quickly to avoid the spray from the fall and from the pool at its base. Beyond lie many spectacular calcite formations. Stalactites, stalagmites, pillars and flowstone border the passage and many of these, forming curious shapes, have been given names by the guides and the visitors. The flowstone is streaked with black and red from lead and iron oxides and an alga causes traces of green. The alga survives using the energy of the electric

. .race through the . . . . air'

light and the carbon dioxide breathed out by visitors to make its own food. From the end of the passage a rocky tunnel continues, and the guide explains that this leads first to a shallow, narrow lake and then to a much larger, deeper one. Long traversed both, the latter by swimming.

On leaving the caves and the car park turn left and drive half a mile. Park tightly at the start of a cart-track that leads over Skirwith moor. Beside the track a footpath sign and a ladder stile indicate your route over the moor to Fell Lane. The moorland pastures of Skirwith support a large number of ewes with lambs. Curlews call and circle overhead before settling to their nests, meadow pipits flutter upwards, swallows scream as they race through the warm afternoon air, plovers wheel and dive and call and rabbits sunbathe and frolic among the celandines and violets.

You climb two more ladder stiles before reaching Fell Lane. Turn left for Ingleborough and follow the deeply rutted cart-track that runs between limestone walls. The verges support celandines, milkmaids, wild strawberry, coltsfoot, wood sorrel, saxifrage, bird's-foot trefoil and the pretty water avens. From beyond the wall a skylark rises, singing, far into the blue sky. The lane ends with a gate and beyond lies Ingleborough, distant in the summer heat, scarred with the feet of many walkers and dotted with tiny figures trailing upwards.

Celandines and bird's foot trefoil

45

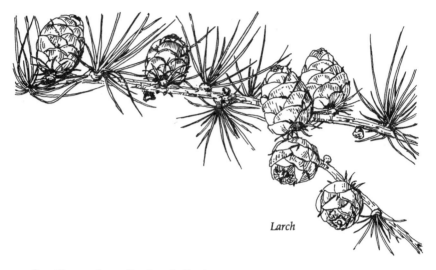

Larch

Continue along the track that now swings out onto Ingleborough Common. Pass the cottage on the left that snuggles against the towering limestone outcrops above. Around it grow larch, oak, ash and beech - all but ash decked with delicate green leaves.

Beyond the cottage the way continues upwards. Spend a little time exploring the limestone outcrops. Among the boulders spleenwort, parsley fern, hart's tongue, wood sorrel, violet and wild strawberry flower. From a solitary hawthorn comes the loud, emphatic song of a wren. Perhaps from this tree came the berry that gave life to a tiny bush thriving in a small hollow in a limestone boulder nearby.

From now on the way is steeply upwards. Bilberry leaves, newly emerged, glow red among the moorland grass. Wheatears flit from boulder to boulder. Move away from the path on the slope near the top and look for wood sorrel, violets and pearlwort sheltering among the mountain boulders.

Reaching the top, you feel the full force of the easterly wind. The favourite windbreak is a stone seat which has four sections looking out onto all quarters. On top is a metal plate detailing the mountains all around, near and far.

Walk to the rim of the summit. Far below lies Batty Moss Viaduct.

Whernside and Pen y ghent stand close by Ingleborough - the Three Peaks. Under all three lie many caves cut by underground streams similar to White Scar Caves.

Ingleborough

Mill Gill
48

9. Mill Gill Force and Whitfield Gill Force, Askrigg, Wensleydale

MR 939915, 935923,   4 miles

PARK IN ONE of the many spaces around the church in the market square of Askrigg and visit St. Oswald's, a large late Perpendicular church with a splendid wooden beamed ceiling. Look at the seventeenth and eighteenth century houses built of warm-brown stone, packed tightly along the winding main street, glowing in the bright May sunshine. Note the early nineteenth century market cross close by the church wall. On this wall a signboard points the direction to take for Mill Gill Force.

Walk along the road and continue when it becomes a track, with comfrey, milkmaids and white deadnettle growing in its verge. Pass through a wicket gate beneath a signpost to a paved path across a buttercup meadow. Walk through a gap in the wall at the end of the path and continue along a track beside the river where bird's eye, kingcups, water avens and ransoms flourish.

Cross a narrow bridge over the tumbling beck and step through a gap in the wall. Turn right and walk to the edge of the wood where another signpost directs the walker to the falls. Follow the path that keeps close beside a wall, with bluebell-covered slopes descending sharply to the hurrying water below. Swallows wheel and scream overhead and a tree pipit ascends from the topmost branch of a larch and descends trilling musically as it returns to the same perch. A garden warbler gives a loud alarm call as the walker comes too near to its territory and a wren sings

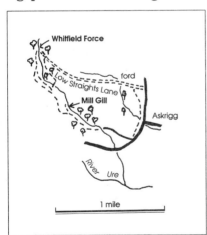

49

Whitfield Force

strongly from foliage close to the river. Small clumps of wood anemones glow paley white among the sweet-smelling carpet of bluebells. Lofty beeches tower upwards adorned with delicate soft-green leaves below which grow male ferns.

Where the path divides take the lower path, well signposted, into a sheer-sided limestone ravine. Ahead lies the magnificent Mill Gill Force, whose water once powered three mills downstream. The slender waterfall descends through a deep cleft in the amphitheatre of bare limestone. Long streams of droplets sparkle and shimmer as they catch the bright sunshine. Wide layers of limestone in steep steps protrude into the hurrying water and spray ricochets into the air. The higher layers of the ravine overhang, devoid of vegetation, and here pairs of jackdaws attend, with much to-ing and fro-ing, to the needs of their clamouring young. Towards the gill bottom the ground slopes more gently and great mats of vegetation, saxifrage, forget-me-nots and ferns, grow luxuriantly in the continual spray. Sycamores, alders, rowans and silver birch lean over this glorious hollow and resound with the songs of blue tits, chaffinches, willow warblers and wrens.

Leave this wonderful corner and return to the division of the path, and follow the signpost directions for Whitfield Gill Force. Walk along the narrow path, bordered with violets and bluebells. A stile gives access to pastures with ewes and lambs and a splendid view of silvery outcrops of Whitfield Scar. Pass through several more man-made gaps in walls, following the well-trodden path. The way comes close to some pretty falls and then the walker passes through a summery glade where willow warblers sing and the beck descends in yet more foaming falls. Kingcups grow close to the water and bluebells and shirtbuttons below the trees.

Where the path divides again take the upper path signposted to Whitfield Gill Force. Walk along the bluebell-bordered path beneath more lofty beeches. This high-level path avoids a very wet area, but as soon as this is passed drop down the steep slope to the side of the river, using a narrow winding downhill track. Clamber along the rocky path to the foot of the magnificent waterfall. A curtain of water descends for thirty feet over a dark brown semicircle of narrowly layered gritstone. Two huge beeches stand at the top and, half-way down the fall, a dipper has built its nest in a hole behind the sparkling streamers of water. At the bottom the water cascades over a mass of mossy rocks before falling into a deep brown pool. Here on a fallen tree stump the dipper pauses before flying up into its nest. Sunlight floods into this secluded hollow where the lush vegetation hosts a myriad of small birds. A grey wagtail flies upstream; a flash of yellow and it is gone. A wren busily enters and re-enters a hole among the rocks of the riverbank feeding its brood. An orange-tip butterfly flits through the warm air of the gill.

Return to the division of the path and take the other path signposted Straits Lane and Askrigg. Cross the narrow bridge just above a waterfall foaming down a series of narrow steps in the bed of Whitfield Beck. Climb the path through the trees on the other side and follow the path as it continues beside the wall. Walk on, climbing steadily until Whitfield Gill Force lies below, its long tresses of water sparkling through the young foliage of the trees. The path crosses an open area and comes to a wicket gate giving access to Straits Lane, a wide cart-track that runs for nearly a mile between limestone walls. From this track there are wide extensive views across the pastures to Addlebrough. Milkmaids, violets, celandines and kingcups line the edges of this lovely walk. Cross the ford and at the end of the track turn right and walk downhill into Askrigg.

' - on a fallen tree stump a dipper pauses"

Gaping Gill
54

10. Gaping Gill and the Reginald Farrer Trail, Ingleborough

MR 751726 - 750699, 5 miles

TAKE THE road signposted Clapham that turns off the A65 and park in the large public car park. Walk through the village, crossing one of the four bridges that span the beck. Walk up the narrow lane beside the hurrying water to where the road turns left. Follow a footpath that leads off to the right, signposted Ingleborough Cave. The track passes between walls and the verges below are filled with June flowers. Cow parsley grows tall and resplendent, herb robert provides bright patches of colour and crosswort grows in great profusion among dog's mercury, now heavy with small green fruits.

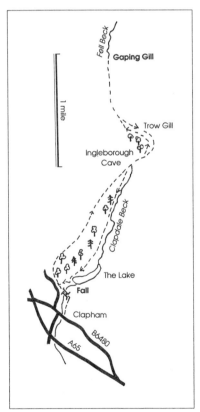

Continue climbing steadily uphill, the beech and sycamore overhead giving way to ash and hawthorn - the latter laden with creamy blossoms. Wood avens, bird's eye, bugle, wild strawberry, violets, bluebells and the pretty water avens flourish in the extra light reaching the grassy edges of the track. From the depths of most of the hawthorns a lesser whitethroat proclaims its territory. Away to the right the limestone outcrops appear white as the sun shines on Norber.

Pass through the gate at Clapdale Farm and turn right as

directed by the signpost. Follow the track as it drops steeply downhill. Turn left at the bottom, joining the track that runs beside the beck and leads to Ingleborough Cave. Stand on the tiny bridge beyond and notice the beck issuing from Clapham Beck Cave, a cavern at the foot of a limestone cliff. Beside the tumbling water stands a dead tree and on the lower lip of a huge knothole a pair of spotted flycatchers assiduously attend their brood, unconcerned by the large number of people queuing to enter the show cave.

'tree pipits ascend'

Walk along the good path as it passes between sheltering wooded slopes where tree pipits ascend into the warm air and a redstart sings its short happy song from a branch of an ash. As the path turns into Trow Gill the slopes become steeper and closer to the path. Great tits, chaffinches and blackcaps call from the mass of trees and shrubs that crowd the top of the gill. Then the limestone faces rear up too sharply for vegetation to grow and the gill becomes chill where the sun does not penetrate. Ascend the steep rocky track that passes through a narrow gap in the huge wall of limestone at the end of the gill.

From now the path becomes muddy but easy to follow. Climb the wooden throughs in the wall onto the open fell where the air is filled with the song of meadow pipits. Ahead lies the path to Little Ingleborough and Ingleborough itself. Look to the left for the interesting blocks of limestone (clints) with hollows and gaps between filled with vegetations (grykes). Beyond, on the same side of the path, is a deep, wooded hollow with a pot-hole at its base. Follow an indistinct track that swings off to the right and just over a small fold in the moor lie the tents of the caving club whose members divert the Fell Beck and organise the 365-feet descent by bo's'n's chair to the bottom of Gaping Gill.

The descent can be made during the spring and August bank holidays. Get there early, pay the fee and receive a numbered disc. Then eat your lunch while waiting for your turn. Don waterproofs before you are strapped into the chair and then the fantastic journey begins. As you descend keep legs tucked beneath you and your head up because the sheer rock face is very close. Wood sorrel glows pearly white in the increasing dark but plants are soon left behind. Then the sides are gone and you descend rapidly through a cloud of spray into a vast black void. There is a slight bump and you are down.

The cave is huge, reputed to be large enough to hold York Minster. Into it, in a long wide veil of sparkling water, descends Fell Beck. Another magnificent waterfall drops from a fissure in the vaulted roof. Both fill the cavern with noise and spray. A lamp, installed by the cavers, gives enough light to explore and to observe the layered patterning on the walls. The floor of the cave, under forty feet of water in the winter, is littered with huge round rocks like enormous pebbles. There are rivers of glutinous mud and mounds of firmer but very sticky clay but all the time one's eye is drawn to the dramatic falls of water and the equally dramatic disappearance of the waters into the floor of the cave. They are the waters of Fell Beck, which was seen earlier re-emerging at

Wood anemones

57

Clapham Beck Cave.

On the journey back up the winch-line look to the right, gaining a wonderful view of the extensiveness of the cave. At the top notice the heather, saxifrage, herb robert, rowan, bilberry, ferns, liverworts, wood sorrel, water avens and wood anemones that surround the entrance and a grey wagtail that darts over the great hole, catching insects for its young.

Return across the moor, where tormentil flowers, to the throughs in the wall. Take the track bearing away to the left where you pass some splendid shake-holes and where cotton grass flies banners of white feathery seeds. Continue past clints and grykes to the edge of Trow Gill enjoying a spectacular view down into the limestone ravine. Rejoin the path walked earlier that leads to the bridge, the flycatchers and the show cave. Refreshments can be obtained here.

Walk on to the gate across the path that gives access to the Reginald Farrer Nature Trail, part of the Ingleborough Estate (now owned by a descendant of Reginald Farrer). From now on the wide, easy-to-walk track passes through bluebell woodland where wild strawberry flowers in vast numbers, wild garlic grows in carpets of white and the pretty woodruff flourishes. Here, too thrive water avens, and two cranesbill - one a delicate pink and the other a very dark purple. From the trees come the songs of chaffinches, willow warblers, mistle thrushes and blackbirds. Far below to the left the Clapham Beck tumbles and sparkles through this lovely woodland. The track continues below many lofty beeches and then passes a mass of rhododendrons in flower, some white, some pink and some red. Through these magnificent bushes the beck tumbles in a foaming waterfall. Look for the unusual trees planted years ago by Reginald Farrer.

Follow the path as it continues beside the artificial lake formed by damming the beck where huge old yews lean over the still brown water. At the end of the lake the path zig-zags downhill. Look for the wooden stile in the wire fence on the left, just before a store for fencing posts. This stile gives access to a little path down to the foot of a lovely waterfall. The beck, on leaving the lake, drops in an elegant curtain of water beneath an arch. It cascades over huge boulders in the river bed where a dipper runs in and out of the foaming water and a grey wagtail races across rocks after insects.

On the other side of the lively beck stands the church of St. James. This lovely corner with its delightful fall tumbling into a wooded ravine contrasts sharply with the austere setting of Gaping Gill where the beck makes its earlier descent.

Bluebell and wild garlic

11. Yordas Cave, Kingsdale

MR 707790, ½ mile

L EAVE THE A65 west of Ingleton following the signs for Thornton in Lonsdale. After driving through the village take the right turn beyond the church and continue for three and a half miles in the direction of Dent. On either side of the road that runs through the lonely, secluded Kingsdale lie limestone scars with bright green turf interspersed with boulders.

Yordas Cave lies hidden among elms, oaks, rowan, Scots pine and beech on the left of the road, the only clump of trees on the roadside since Thornton. Park on the verge close by and enter the woodland by a gate. Walk up the dry bed of a beck - ignoring what might appear to be the entrance but is really a very large nettle bed - to the real entrance twenty feet further on and higher up. It has a bricked arch built into the natural opening.

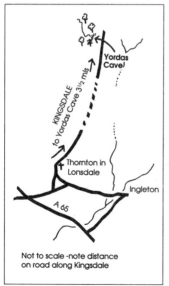

Not to scale -note distance
on road along Kingsdale

The writer went equipped with wellington boots and a powerful torch but on entering was astounded by an array of candles placed in natural niches around the cave. A young teacher had taken her charges into the cave and they had placed the candles, turning it into a fairy grotto.

Walk to the far right-hand corner and climb up into an inner cave, where a foot or so of water covers the pebbly bottom. Here a most spectacular fall descends fifty feet or more, dropping onto a rock which diverts the flow to the left, making it spout into the air. It then plummets in a wide wall of water splashing onto the pebbles filling the cave with spray

'go in search of the source'

and noise.

Return to the large cave and look at the fascinating patterning of the limestone. Flowstone, covered with moisture, forms extraordinary symmetrical shapes. Stalactites hang from the roof. Tiny drips of water sparkle in the torchlight as they fall from rock formations. Large river boulders, fixed in position with limestone mortar, form the roof of a small side cave.

After viewing the dramatic fall it is good to go in search of the source of the water. Leave the cave and scramble up the dry bed to the foot of a small waterfall. Here the beck tumbles through elms, rowans and beeches. It passes crevices filled with hart's tongue ferns and ransoms still in bud. It then flows into a deep pot, dropping down and down and disappearing from sight, reappearing in the inner cavern to thrill onlookers with its spectacular plunge.

Gunnerside Gill

12. Gunnerside Gill, Swaledale

MR 935030, 7¹/₂ miles

G REAT KNAPWEED rears up huge purple heads to the sun and large clumps of water avens redden the roadside verges of Swaledale and Wensleydale in the middle of June. Vast numbers of golden buttercups replace the bright green pastures of May and among them grow sorrel and a pretty mauve cranesbill. Strong limestone walls box in this glorious profusion and sturdy, well-maintained barns dot the pastures, a pleasing vista stretching away to the foot of the stern rounded slopes of the Pennines.

Park on the west side of the beck in the middle of the village of Gunnerside. Walk over the bridge and continue a few yards to the sloping green surrounded by cottages where once lived the miners who worked in the lead mines in the gills above the village. This small, compact settlement, built of local stone with no intrusion of white painted walls or jarring modern architecture, glows warmly in the morning sunshine.

Return to the beck and follow the signpost directions to Gunnerside Gill. The path keeps close to the racing water for most of the long walk to Blakethwaite. Buttercups, pink clover and cow parsley border the path and dog roses turn soft pink heads

Old mine workings

'dog roses turn soft pink heads to the sun'

to the sun. Turn right and climb stone steps as directed, pass through a gate and continue around beside a wall. In the pasture to the right of the path crosswort, milkmaids and milk thistle flower. Follow the well-marked track through a wicket gate into Birbeck Wood where wood avens, wild strawberry and cranesbill blossom. Hazel, ash and blackthorn are the haunts of young willow warblers and chaffinches, and from the undergrowth comes the loud, emphatic song of a wren. A cuckoo calls frequently but does not show itself.

Pass through another wicket gate and climb more steps to where a rowan laden with creamy blossoms plays host to a family of redstarts. Rich-red tails flash among the leaves as the birds flit with jerky flight from branch to branch; occasionally dark black below the eye and white above reveal the presence of the male. Follow the path as it drops out of the wood to a small dell beneath alders where marsh marigolds grow.

Continue along the well-marked path through gaps in walls. Sometimes the path is on the open fell and is covered with tormentil and bedstraw, where meadow pipits soar into the summer air. At others it passes through the remains of earlier industry. Here are entrances to old mine workings, spoil tips, floors with no walls and arches with no roofs. But nature has softened this industrial dereliction with soft turf spangled with wild thyme, crosswort, bird's eye, bugle, Tom Thumb and a pearly white saxifrage.

Follow the track through a stile, climbing a shady slope where hard fern grows resplendent with upright fertile fronds and bright green prostrate infertile ones. Pass through the gap in the wall onto the open fell, which is alive with scuttling rabbits. Wheatears scold as the walker comes too near to their young and red grouse call from the heather close by. In small, wet areas about the path brooklime thrives, orange-tip butterflies flit ahead and large, glossy black beetles sunbathe on rocks. It is an idyllic scene today and it is difficult to envisage the privations of the miners of yesterday who had to walk this route in all winds and weather before and after a long, arduous day's work wresting ore from Gunnerside Gill.

'orange-tip butterflies

Walk on uphill and look across to a lovely waterfall tumbling through the verdant Botcher Gill. The way continues as a wide grassy swathe through low-growing bracken. On the other side of the gill lie huge tips of mine spoil pushed out from the stone-built turreted exits of the Dolly Lead level. Above the path towers the pale grey face of Swina Bank Scar.

The path now leads you into a lunar landscape with dramatic

evidence of the labour of innumerable workmen. Spoil tips, roofless buildings, entrances to dark tunnels, steps up and steps down litter the slopes. And then there are the hushes - deep gouges in the hillside down which raced great torrents of water released by miners from artificial dams above. The water washed away all in its path revealing the veins of lead beneath. Here must have been shouting and the noise of machinery. Today all is quiet except for the sharp peep, peep, peep of a ring ousel angry at the presence of a hungry peregrine. It calls for a long time, sitting on a wall of the disused Lownathwaite lead mine, its gorget sparkling white, its plaintive call echoing back from the steep slopes.

Where there is a choice of path take the upper one for a spectacular overall view of the mine. In rock crevices about the path spleenwort grows and common speedwell dapples the ground with soft mauve. Continue along the path as it drops to a charming waterfall that cascades in foaming white tresses over a drop in the bed of the beck.

From the waterfall the path begins to ascend the steep slopes above a ravine through which the Gunnerside tumbles in glorious waterfalls, partially obscured by rowans heavy with blossom. On the far side the sheer limestone scar is aptly named Eweleap. Above the ravine lies another delightful fall, the glory of this one unobscured by rock walls or trees. Grouse call from clumps of heather and another ring ousel scolds from a nearby boulder.

Scramble across the foot of Cross Gill, down which tumble more elegant waterfalls, and continue along the rough path into Blakethwaite Gill. From here you have a first glimpse of the man-made fall ahead. It flows from the higher of the two dams in the gill, the upper one intact and the lower one breeched. The breeched dam lies below you. All trace of the dammed water has gone but in the beck a pair of dippers feed busily. A narrow track ascends steeply and then the fall lies ahead. Climb up to the ridge and look over the bleak moorland that stretches into the distance. The beck winds its way across the moor and fills a deep pool above the fall. Then it races through a small gap in the dam and hurtles down a ladder of stone steps, streaming in a myriad of droplets sparkling in the sunshine. Overhead hang blossoming rowan. Juniper and bilberry grow low on the enfolding sides and butterwort leaves star the muddy sides. The falling water drops into a basin and rages on

Curlew - 'a pair fly overhead'

over a tumble of sandstone boulders. This is the territory of a pair of grey wagtails and the place to eat your lunch.

To return, walk back along the rough path past Cross Gill and the ravine overlooked by Eweleap Scar to just below the waterfall on the Gunnerside. Cross the beck by convenient boulders, by the various bridges built many years ago and still sound, or by a more recent bridge of boulders. Spend some time here looking at the derelict buildings, at the soundly constructed arches that give entrance to the levels, at the strong retaining walls and at the beautifully-built furnace shaped like a beehive.

Cross the beck issuing from Blind Gill and walk on along the wide grassy path ahead. From here look down on the splendid falls at the confluence of the Blind and Gunnerside Becks. This is a delightful high level walk with extensive views of the gill far below and Yorkshire stretching away into the haze. Meadow brown butterflies flit ahead and grouse call from the heather.

The path joins a cart-track by the magnificent waterfall at the head of Botcher Gill. Walk over the steep slope using sheep tracks to see it in its full glory as it descends in great haste over natural steps between huge blocks of sandstone before streaming away under rowan and bird cherry. Pass through the gate and continue along the track to where there is another splendid view of the waterfall. Close by the track a mother grouse stands on a heather plant, wattle raised, crowing loudly in her endeavours to keep her seven curious youngsters together. They scurry hither and thither, cheeping happily, unworried by the walker's intrusion into their territory.

The cart-track swings out onto the moor and the nesting ground of the curlew. A pair fly overhead calling quietly to each other, another walks across the track and several give their bubbling call from higher on the slopes. Cotton-grass waves its fluffy seeds, lousewort grows close to the path and the drier turf is colourful with saxifrage, Tom Thumb and wood anemone. A cuckoo - perhaps the same one - calls from Birbeck Wood below.

Where the cart-track swings to the right look for a path, indistinct at first, that continues straight ahead in the direction of Gunnerside, which snuggles in a fold at the foot of the fells. From this path can be seen many of the thousands of rabbits that enjoy the peace and quiet of the gill. Look for the odd black one that shows up so clearly against the short turf. This track leads to a wicket gate in a wall and a short slope down to the centre of the village.

. . . . 'another walks across the track'

Cliff Beck beyond Muker

13. Ellas's Stot Wood and Muker, Swaledale

MR 933985, 896979,   1¹/₂ miles

AFTER SEVERAL days of heavy rain the River Swale flows very fast and is chocolate coloured. When the sun shines once more, the rain-washed air becomes lambent.

To reach Ellas's Stot Wood leave the B6270 at Gunnerside by a narrow road which runs over the fell in a westerly direction, on the northern side of the River Swale. Just less than a mile from the centre of Gunnerside the lane makes a sharp left turn. Park here just beyond the cattle-grid, close to the racing Ivelet Beck. By the water grows a myriad of summer flowers. Look for St. John's wort, cat valerian, willow herb, meadow sweet, marsh stitchwort, horsetails, water mint, foxglove, orchis, hard-heads and ragged robin thriving in the damp ground. Hazel bushes that crowd the edge of the beck carry a heavy load of nuts and rose bushes a good crop of hips. Honeysuckle, with large sweet-smelling creamy blossoms, clambers over neighbouring vegetation.

Cross the road. Walk back up the steep slope of the road and then step onto the fell. Bear to the left, following the edge of the wood. Here the white scuts of rabbits seem to be everywhere. The dog is so bewildered that it does not know which way to run and is even more puzzled when it meets a tiny rabbit running towards it as it returns in response to our whistle. Here on the edge of the wood

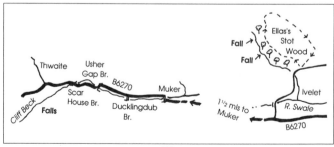

Willow herb, meadow sweet and water mint

the air is heavy with the scent of elderflowers.

The path climbs steadily, giving the walker a wonderful view of Swaledale bathed in sunshine. A curlew flies overhead, calling plaintively. Cross a small beck that dances merrily through hawthorn and rowan bushes alive with the songs of wrens, chaffinches and tits. A spotted flycatcher feeds a pleading youngster. Flashes of fiery red tails reveal the presence of a pair of redstarts. A young willow warbler flits through the branches, the yellow of its breast catching the sunlight. Above the water, wild roses blossom and foxgloves flower about the banks of the little beck.

Just beyond this lovely corner follow the indistinct path that bears away to the left, following the edge of the wood. To the right, over the fell a kestrel hovers, regularly dropping down and being momentarily lost to sight among the tough moorland grass as it hunts for prey.

From here look back to the road over the Buttertubs Pass snaking up the far hillside. Continue along the thin track as it passes through bracken. Where the path descends a grassy landslip, clamber down

71

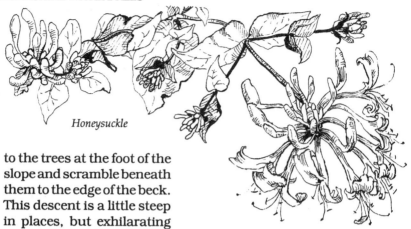

Honeysuckle

to the trees at the foot of the
slope and scramble beneath
them to the edge of the beck.
This descent is a little steep
in places, but exhilarating
to do. Here in spring primroses brighten the slopes, to be followed
by a carpet of bluebells.

At the edge of the beck turn right and move upstream to the foot
of a magnificent fall. The Ivelet Beck thunders down the steep drop
in its bed in one long fall of foaming, roaring water. No trace of peat
stain or chocolate colour is visible here. The furious water then
rages on through this secluded deciduous woodland to pass under
the bridge by the cattle-grid where you have parked.

Return up the steep slope, disturbing yet more rabbits, to the
tiny track. Turn left, passing through more bracken which, in
turn, gives way to heather, now laden with pale pink flowers.
Continue to the end of the wood where the beck descends in
another pretty fall. Return across the moorland, keeping parallel
with the edge of the wood, until the road is regained.

Walk back to the car and drive on, then descend the narrow road
into the hamlet of Ivelet. Drive with extreme care down the narrow
road beyond the houses and beside the surging Swale. Cross the
narrow pack-horse bridge and park among the trees on the right.
This splendid bridge arches exquisitely high above the swirling
water. Until the nineteenth century ponies carried lead from local
mines across the bridge. Look for the corpse stones on which
coffins were placed by pall bearers pausing on their way to
consecrated ground.

Drive on once more and at the end of the lane turn right onto the
B6270 and drive into Muker - always a lovely village in which to

Ivelet Bridge

idle an hour or so. Stroll out of the village, crossing Usha Gap Bridge and walking until the lovely waterfall on Cliff Beck is seen to the left. Look for a gap in the wall, just beyond a farm gate. Pass through and walk across the meadow, where Friesian bullocks graze, to the foot of the fall. Here the rushing water descends over rock steps and ledges in a mass of foam and spray, beneath shading sycamores and rowans. This is a beautiful waterfall, different in form and height from the one visited earlier. It is easy to walk to and comes as a reward after all the hard scrambling to see the earlier one.

Coffin stone - Ivelet Bridge

73

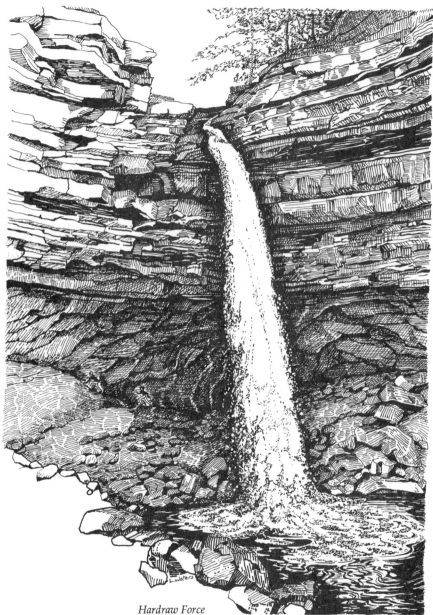

Hardraw Force

14.   Hardraw Force, Wensleydale

MR 869915,   1 mile

L EAVE THE A684, one and a half miles west of Hawes at a turn signposted Hardrow. At the village, leave the car on a parking space opposite the Green Dragon Inn and buy a ticket for viewing the force. The inn is close by the Church of St. Mary and St. John, a plain building with large yews in front and the sound of the falls behind. Hardrow village has a quiet charm and a farm in its midst.

Go through the inn and continue along the footpath, leaving the churchyard on the left. In the middle of August the verges of the path are full of late-summer flowers. Vast stands of rose-bay willow-herb provide patches of deep pink that blend with hardheads, woundwort, milk thistle and pink clover. A gateway in an ancient wall is shaded by a conifer. Pass through and walk straight ahead. A huge sweet chestnut leans over a grassy patch and here grow yarrow, meadow sweet, harebell, herb robert, buttercup, parsley and stitchwort. To the left of the path, on the other side of a stream, a steep limestone cliff towers, almost hidden beneath a magnificent cloak of trees. Ashes grow tall and in great abundance, finding footholds for their roots in the many crevices between the layers of rock. Lofty Scots pines grow at the top. The right side of the path is deeply shaded by another almost perpendicular rock face. This, too, is richly clad in vegetation and in the moist fissures that run down to the path wood sorrel, moss and liverworts flourish. Close by the path wood avens, herb robert and canterbury bell, a garden escapee now well established, thrive.

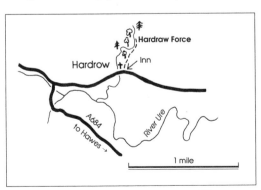

After a five-minute walk the spectacular fall lies ahead. It tumbles through a gap in the rim of a rocky amphitheatre and as you stand amazed at such magnificence you begin to realise that you have walked into a huge hollow and that the cliffs on either side of the approach path swing round and become one. The stream plummets for a hundred feet in one continuous fall of white foam. Towards the bottom it falls onto soft, shaly rocks and cascades on to more before raging into a wide shallow pool. Luxuriating in the constant spray grow elms, sycamores and alders. Behind the long white plume of water grow clumps of golden saxifrage, and from the fissures in the layered rocks hang the strap-shaped fronds of hart's tongue fern.

The lip of this impressive waterfall was destroyed in a disastrous flood late in the last century. An artificial one was put in its place by the workmen of Lord Wharncliffe, the landowner at that time.

'a gateway in an ancient wall'

L.Waters.

Cotter Force

77

15. Cotter Force, Wensleydale

MR 848919, 1 mile

PARK IN THE lay-by close by Holme Head Bridge on the A684
two miles north-west of Hawes. The signpost to the force is
painted green, merging with the vegetation, and is easy to miss.
The path to the force keeps beside the sweetly flowing Cotterdale
Beck, with a wire fence separating the path from farmland beyond.
The row of barbed wire along the top of the fence is the only jarring
note on a lovely walk. The river bank is lined with ash, alder,
sycamore, rowan and elm and from these comes the boy-like
whistle of the tree creeper. Swallows swoop overhead, delighting
in the myriad of flies which have matured all at once on the hot
mid-August day. The insects delight also a pair of spotted
flycatchers, which make rapid sorties into the air after their prey,
returning each time to their familiar bare branch - the lowest
branch of the tree. Blue tits chuckle in the alders and a wren

whistles its strong vibrant
song, from low in the
vegetation of the river bank.
The glowing red-purple
flowers of betony and hard-
head crowd the river bank.
Climb through the stile
and continue walking along
the riverside. The sun slants

Stile

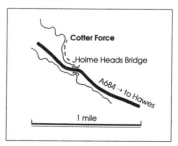

through the trees and sunbeams make the water sparkle like crystal where it foams and falls around boulders in its way. On a boundary wall a corncrake walks with head well down, lifting its feet high as it goes. It flies down into the grass beyond the wall, its bill yellow in the sunlight, its flanks barred and its wings a rich chestnut. Soon it returns to the wall and is joined by another, and both slender birds, with necks drawn in, move on along the wall unworried by pied wagtails hawking flies overhead.

After half a mile the graceful waterfall can be seen sparkling through the trees. The beck tumbles over the layered rock and rages down three large steps before it falls in one long drop. It falls again, then races over more rocky ledges before dropping several feet into a deep, peat-stained pool. The August sun sends dancing sunbeams across the foaming water, and their reflections move across the layered rocks beside the pool. On either side of the force the water has cut away small caves and large rocks overhang the brown water that surges into the dark recesses.

On the banks bordering the water, wood sage, en-chanter's nightshade, canterbury bell, herb robert, meadow sweet and wood sorrel grow. Delicate ferns clothe the steep slopes of the rock faces and various species of liverwort and moss adhere to any wet surface. Two dragonflies flit across the water, their gossamer wings catching the sunlight.

Wren, Knapweed and betony

79

Ash and elm lean over the water and ivy, with large glossy leaves, clings to rock faces and tree trunks. High above the fall a narrow footbridge crosses the roaring water, but here the path ends.

Sit on the large, flat rocks above the Cotterdale as it flows on its way after its joyous leap. Enjoy this fairy grotto, which is filled with the sound of falling water and where dappled sunlight reveals nature's abundance.

Wood Sorrel

Hoggarth's Leap, River Swale

16.   River Swale West of Keld, Swaledale

MR 893015, 894014,   1 mile

T HE VILLAGE OF Keld hugs the south bank of the Swale. A tiny cluster of stone cottages surrounds several imposing buildings, two of which recall an era before television filled so many evening hours. The literary institute stands on one side of a tiny square which also contains the school - built in 1842 but closed, alas, in the 1970s - and the imposing United Reform Church, rebuilt in 1860. Just below these splendid buildings, on the other side of the road, stands the public hall and reading room, now little used and in need of some love and care. Beyond the hall follow the road round to the left. Ahead lies a gate to the left of a cattle-shed which gives access to a track that runs down to the river bank. Follow the noise of roaring water.

Continue along a narrow path that heads upstream between meadow sweet and the lovely yellow wild balsam. Stand on a tiny knoll beneath the trees for the best view of Hoggarth's Leap. The

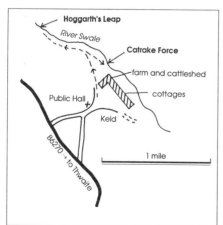

River Swale comes down, steep rocky step after steep rocky step, in roaring white falls richly stained with peat. The tremendous noise and the delightful setting is an experience not to be missed. After this display of fury the beck surges on, deep, dark and wide beneath heavily wooded slopes of birch and ash.

Walk back along the path and continue on beside the river past the track to the

82

farm. Ahead the roaring tumult of falling water pinpoints Catrake Force. Once steps led down to these falls but they have been washed away and you cannot reach the river side. But if you are sure of foot continue with great care along the muddy and slippery path that runs at the edge of the cliff. Look down through ash, hazel, sycamore and birch to the falls below. The highest fall spreads the whole width of the beck. The lower one, channelled more tightly between projecting boulders, roars furiously at the hindrance in its passage through a gorge. The gorge lies behind the farm and the row of cottages at the foot of the village.

Above the path a steep, grassy sward rich in summer flowers sweeps steeply upwards. Hard-heads, purple vetch, wood avens, scabious, harebells and small flowered cranesbill carpet the turf. Overhead blue tits, robins and chaffinches move through the trees, their calls silenced by the great sound of the Swale.

You can leave your car on the verge-side in the village, but the few spaces are soon filled. It is better to park on one of the many small lay-bys on the B6270 and walk down the short lane - a dead-end - to the village.

Vetch

83

East Gill Force

84

17. River Swale East of Keld, Swaledale

MR 898010, 2¹/₂ miles

L EAVE YOUR CAR on a convenient verge on the B6270 and walk down either lane signposted Keld Only. Both lanes lead to a row of attractive cottages. To their right a track leads off between hawthorn bushes where young blue tits chuckle and chase each other and a robin scolds. Beneath the hawthorn ragwort, woundwort, small flowered cranesbill, stitchwort, scabious and harebells proclaim that it is August.

Walk on to where there is a two-way Pennine Way sign and the track divides. Take the left fork and pass beneath a leafy arch to a gate onto a grassy area. Here a wooden bridge takes you across the River Swale. Just beyond, the lively beck that races through East Gill joins the Swale after tumbling white-topped over wide, regularly spaced steps of rock. Ash, rowan, beech and willow gracefully shade these charming falls and from the trees, above the sound of the splashing beck, a black cap sings its fine song. It flits from branch to branch enjoying the myriad of midges which plague the walker below.

Beyond the bridge leave the path and walk beside the feeder beck to charming East Gill Force, where silvery, sparkling water falls in long, steep, white curtains. This striking triple fall is easy to miss and to do so would be a loss.

Return to the path and walk uphill to leave the Pennine Way and to join Alfred Wainwright's Coast to Coast footpath. Turn right and cross the bridge over

85

the beck just above the pretty falls now hidden from sight, below, to the right. Continue along the path, which passes onto open pasture along the flanks of Beldi Hill. To the right lies the lovely Kisdon Gorge, its steep sides clad in lush deciduous vegetation densely hiding, but not deadening, the River Swale negotiating Kisdon Force. A small flock of goldfinches chatter conversationally as they fly to the trees on the other side of the gorge. A wren sings boldly from a bracken frond and then disappears, mouse-like, when disturbed.

Enjoy this high-level walk as it leaves the pastures behind and passes into woodland on either side. Blackbirds and mistle thrushes feed voraciously in the rowans which are laden with a rich crop of berries. The birds blunder noisily and clumsily through the branches as if drunk on the juice of the berries.

'tumbling over steps of rock'

As the gorge opens out, ahead lies a lovely moorland view of softly rounded slopes, vivid green in the bright sun with a trace of mist hanging over the meandering river far below. Stay on the main track, by the wall, which drops steeply downwards -

the Coast to Coast footpath forking left towards the ruined Crackpot Hall. In an open area a dozen rabbits bask in the warm sun.

The path comes to a bridge over Swinner Gill Beck. Beside the water stand the remains of a building that was in use when lead was mined, once a profitable industry. Just above the ruin the beck descends through ragwort, angelica, golden rod, pennywort, bracken, small hawthorns and stunted birch in splendid falls over wide rock steps. If time permits cross the bridge over the beck and walk on to the village of Muker. If not return the same way until you reach the two-way Pennine Way sign once more. Here turn left away from the village and walk for a quarter of a mile.

The path is tree-lined and richly bordered in flowers, from which an excellent view is obtained of the attractive East Gill Force. Several young spotted flycatchers dart from bare branches into the insect-laden air above the open ground beyond. A signpost directs the way down the gorge side to Kisdon Upper Force. Follow

Black-cap

the narrow path as it winds through ash, oak and rowan beneath towering crags and around tumbled boulders. Here flourish lady's mantle, canterbury bell, crosswort, forget-me-nots and yellow bedstraw. Pigeons fly off over the tree-tops, disturbed from their feasting on acorns. As the path nears the beck bear to the left and follow the trod down to the waterside for a good view of the Upper Force.

If wearing good strong footwear continue. Follow the narrow track as it bears left. It is a well defined but slightly hazardous path high on a steep slope above the Swale. It crosses a soil slip and then winds downhill with many an exposed root to trip over or to use to advantage to reach the Lower Force. The view upstream is a great reward.

The Swale comes through the gorge and descends the rocky steps that form the Upper Force. The water frothing and foaming, and stained with peat, turns golden as it catches the sunlight. It drops into a wide, deep, darkly brown small lake surrounded by low walls of layered limestone. The river then surges forward to a narrow exit - the Lower Force - from the large pool. It falls over three steps and plummets downwards in a roaring jet. The wind funnels into the bottom of the raging water, catching the spray and tossing it into the air. And then after this glorious display of petulance the river lazily continues on its way to form the large meanders seen earlier from the path to Swinner Gill.

Sit on the large, flat boulders around the Lower Force and enjoy this lovely, lonely hollow where wild flowers drenched in spray fill the air with fragrance, where trees thrive on the lower slopes and hide the glory of Kisdon Force from the path above, and where the sheer limestone face rears upwards, shining silver in the warm afternoon sun.

18. Aysgarth Falls, Wensleydale
MR 010885 - 017888, 2 miles

F OR EASY ACCESS to the higher, middle and lower falls on the
River Ure, entailing minimum walking on the road, use the
Aysgarth Falls car park. This lies north-east of Aysgarth village
and is well signposted. Parking charges are very reasonable. There
is a National Park information centre, café and toilets.

A signpost indicates the route for the higher falls which leaves
by an exit at the west end. The path passes beneath ash and elm
and through these dance blue tits hunting for insects. Young
chaffinches, undeterred by the heat of an August afternoon, chase
each other through the leaves and into the air.

The path comes close to the road and here woundwort, bramble
and nipplewort thrive. Among these grow wild strawberry plants
laden with tiny lush berries. The sound of the upper falls draws the
walker on to a less wooded area where herb robert, ragwort, self
heal and hard-head brighten the grassy flats. The path leads to a

Aysgarth Falls

large open area where families picnic and dogs run in and out of the water. Smooth flat rocks stretch out into the surging river and from these children paddle and fish.

The very wide, slow moving Ure washes along beside the flat boulders, then plunges downwards in white foam, streaked with brown, onto more wide, flat rocks. It swirls around smaller boulders and then drops down again in frothing foam. The rocky drop in the river bed extends for the whole width of the river and the noise of falling water fills the air.

The track continues upstream to where there are more rapids, less steep but straddling the river. The Ure is chocolate brown here and its shoreline deep in silt. The path runs on a bank several feet above the river and wooded slopes, clad with ash, sycamore and elm, stretch upwards. Enjoy the view upstream.

To visit the middle falls return to the car park and follow the signpost directions. These take the walker along a path to the road and to sturdy gates on the other side. A short walk leads to a path that slopes down through the trees to an excellent viewpoint. In these falls, the whole width of the bed of the Ure drops in steeply stepped rock ridges. Torrents of white and rust-coloured water race downward. In places a film of water slides like liquid glass over the rocky ledges and ridges.

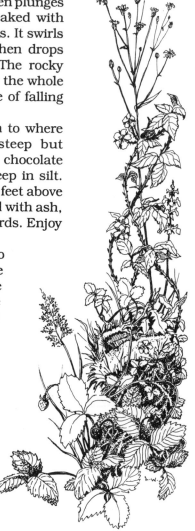

Wild strawberries, bramble, woundwort and nipplewort

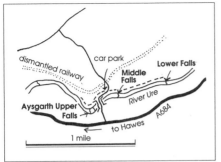

Viewed from above and framed by cherry, oak and sycamore, the middle falls are a wonderful sight.

Above the falls a grey wagtail chases flies on a flat boulder, regularly swooping into the air and onto the bank - perhaps to feed a late brood. Over the noise of the tumbling water can be heard the clock of St. Andrew's, Aysgarth, chiming the hour. Leave these beautiful falls and return to the main path and continue onwards towards the lower falls.

The path passes through mixed deciduous woodland where rowan is laden with bunches of vermilion fruit and honeysuckle trails its fragile branches over much of the vegetation. Beyond a gate the path leads out into an open meadow rich in wild flowers creating a vivid mosaic of colour against a backcloth of seeded grasses, a warm gold in the bright afternoon sun.

Continue along the path as it swings down towards the river. Pass through the trees that border the falls, out onto a small railed area for the best view of the spectacular falls. Here again the river bed drops in a series of wide steps and over these the Ure foams and boils, filling the river valley with sound. Today the water sparkles and dances and flows gracefully on its way, but when in spate the higher, middle and lower falls of the Ure are an awesome sight.

St. Andrew's Church

91

Cauldron Falls, Walden Beck

19. Cauldron Falls, Walden Beck, West Burton, Wensleydale

MR 020867, 150 yards

WIDE GRASSY verges flank the road that runs through the middle of West Burton. The houses and cottages that surround the extensive, elongated green glow a warm soft beige in the August sun. To reach the village take the A684, then turn onto the B6160. If travelling in an easterly direction you want the second right turn off the A road beyond the turning for Aysgarth Falls. In the village leave the B road where it makes a sharp turn away from the noisy Walden Beck. Keep to the narrow lane beside the hurrying water and park your car close to the verge just before the village green. Walk back to a track that leads to your right and down to the beck. The sign to the waterfall is on a wall at the right side of the track and is easy to miss.

Look for some pretty falls below the bridge. Close by the surging water grows a large clump of bloody cranesbill. Walk on a hundred yards more to obtain the best view of the Cauldron Falls which once powered a woollen mill in the village.

The Walden races downhill in a foaming torrent confined in a narrow bed. It spreads, like a curtain of lace, over six wide ledges of rock before descending onto two more shallow ridges, then drops into a deep brown pool. To the left is a huge cave cut out under the layered limestones and to the right a smaller narrow cave. Ash trees hang elegantly over the foaming beck and on either side grow herb robert, hart's tongue fern, wild parsley and feathery moss.

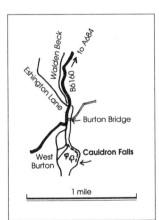

On a large flat boulder projecting into the pool two mallards doze, one standing on one leg with its head in its wing and

Mallards doze

the other sitting on the rock. Today the water in the pool flows gently and the ducks can doze in the sun but when the Walden Beck is in spate the ducks leave and the boulder disappears beneath the raging water.

Hart's tongue fern

Wain Wath Force - Swaledale
95

20. Wain Wath Force, Swaledale

MR 886015, 50 yards

T HE RIVER SWALE flows through wild and lonely fells. Small quiet hamlets and remote farms lie dotted sparsely through the untouched dale. Limestone walls cross fields and slopes, reaching the edge of the river's rich brown turbulent waters. These rage through tree-lined banks and wooded gorges, spectacularly negotiating the many drops in the bed of the Swale on its journey to the sea.

Wain Wath Force is found where the river tumbles in many pretty falls spread laterally along a steep rocky step, each white fall streaked with the beer-coloured stain of peat, which turns to gold as it catches the sun. The fall lies close to the B6270 half a mile north-west of the village of Keld. From ample roadside parking beside the Force, a small gate opens onto the flat rocks below the foaming fall and a little further along the road a stile and some sturdy steps also lead down to the edge of the surging water.

On the far side of the Swale a limestone rock face supports oak, ash, hazel and rowan, with ferns, hawkweed and golden rod flourishing in crevices too small to maintain trees.

Buttercups, scabious, stitchwort, herb robert, meadow sweet and harebells flower in the grassy sward that edges the water.

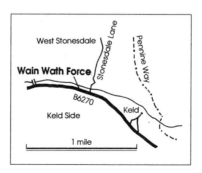

96

Cautley Spout

21. Cautley Spout, Howgills

MR 684975, 3 miles

SOMETIMES in September Yorkshire shows few touches of autumn. The trees along the lanes are clad in dark green leaves, only the horse-chestnuts showing bright banners. Wild flowers colour the verges: hard-heads, rose-bay willow-herb, campion and herb robert provide pinks and mauves; dog daisies, bindweed, meadow sweet and yarrow are pristine white against a green back-cloth; and ragwort's yellow blossoms add a golden glow. But pride of place must be given to the lovely, stately Indian balsam flowering pink and white in great abundance in the roadside ditches.

Cautley Spout can be seen from the road. After several wet days it tumbles in fury down the steep slopes. Leave the car on a verge beyond the Cross Keys Hotel, on the A683, four miles north-east of Sedbergh. From here a signposted footpath leads sharply downwards beneath ash and sycamore to a narrow, wooden bridge over the River Rawthey. The dark brown surging water swirls round the sturdy supports of the bridge and then races on to swell, in time, the water of the Lune. Above the bridge a bright white blob on a rock pinpoints a dipper, its dark umber feathers exquisitely camouflaging the remainder of its body. It stands quite still and gradually the observer can discern the warm chestnut band below its bib. Higher up, the river descends in foaming falls partly obscured by vegetation.

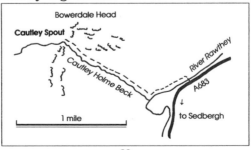

98

Pass through the gate at the end of the bridge and bear left along a clear, reinforced path that follows the route of the river. Here another dipper pauses and preens on a rock and then steps into the water and disappears. In a few second it walks out of the water onto a boulder, bobbing and preening again before setting off to inspect crevices for insects. Tiny streams cross the path and in these wet areas self heal and spearwort flower. Tormentil brightens the fell turf and grows among the bracken. Ahead lie the steep slopes that sweep up to Cautley Crag and to the right sprawls Yarlside, its top veiled in mist.

Along the river bank a host of young meadow pipits dally and disport themselves delaying their departure from the fells for more hospitable climes. Beyond the river, in a meadow belonging to

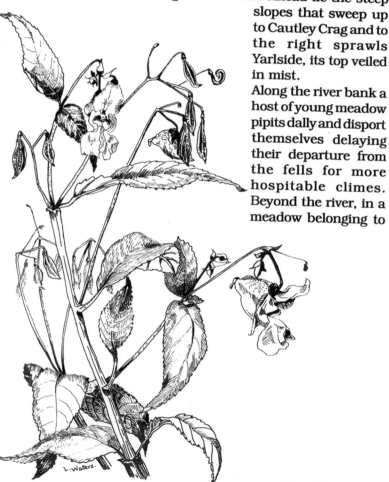

Indian balsam

Cautley Farm, black-headed gulls peck and prod, industriously hunting for prey, unlike the two nearby herons which stand quite still, one-legged, sunbathing and sleeping the afternoon away.

Follow the path as it swings away from the Rawthey. To the left a white-topped beck drops through a tree-clad gill in a series of pretty falls. Below the path the pasture around a fodder-holder attracts a small flock of rooks which assiduously search for insects. More and more of the steep scree slope of Cautley Crag comes into view as the walker moves along the gently rising path towards the waterfall. Dense dark green bracken covers the lower slopes but where it crowds the higher areas of Ben End the fronds are tinged with brown. Rushes with heavy seed heads are now pale fawn. Make time to look back down to the green fields bordered with dark green hedges on the other side of the Rawthey. Beyond, moorland stretches away to the foot of Baugh Fell.

The path has been alternately very wet and then dry through reinforcement. Now it becomes a wide grassy swathe through short bracken. Ahead the magnificent Cautley Beck races down the highest slopes in a thin silvery stream. Then it descends in a wide spectacular cascade that boils and foams, with spray being caught by the wind and tossed high into the air. Below the cascades it rages against the side of a curving lip of rock and breeches this at the lowest part to fall in a broad curtain of water that bounces off a series of projecting ledges. Then the energy of this impetuous beck is channelled through a narrow gap in the rocks to plummet for many, many feet in one splendid jet of sparkling water into a hidden surging pool. And still it tumbles on, foaming and fuming, filling the gorge with noise.

Continue along the path and then, with care, move to the edge of the gorge to see the beauty below. Rowans laden with heavy bunches of vermilion berries and with leaves just tinged with red contrast sharply with the many hollies scattered through the gorge. Ash trees growing tall in the sheltered gill have green leaves - unlike the birches, clad almost entirely in soft yellow.

Below, in the rock gardens, grow verdant mosses and ferns. Ivy with bright shiny leaves trails down the limestone rock face. Angelica heavy with seed, heather in pink flower, hard-heads, lady's mantle, golden rod, all thrive in the continual spray. From here the walker can continue climbing beside the mountain stream to where it descends in more cascades, and can then walk on into Bowderdale.

But when you return to the car park, visit the tiny Wesleyan Methodist Chapel (built in 1845) a mile along the road towards Sedbergh.

'the tiny Wesleyan Methodist chapel'

Black Force
102

22. Black Force, Carlin Gill, Howgills

MR 645993, 4 miles

L EAVE THE A684 which passes through Sedbergh by a side
turn leading northwards, signposted Howgill. Within a mile
this lane leaves the town behind and becomes single track, with
few passing places. The hedgerows that line the lane, making it
seem almost too narrow for a car, are still in full leaf in this third
week of October. The rose trees, glorious when in blossom in the
summer, are now heavily laden with scarlet hips. Blackthorn has
a heavy crop of sloes and juicy blackberries glow glossily in the
welcome sunshine. Scattered along the lane are many ash saplings
just mature enough to have formed large bunches of papery,
brown keys. Pink campion, herb robert, foxgloves and hawkweed
colour the verges, flowering on into the end of the year in this
sheltered environment.

The Quaker Chapel and Beckfoot Viaduct lie to the left of the lane
and the smooth grassy slopes of the high fells tower up to the right.
After crossing Fairmile Beck the lane becomes an unfenced track
across the skirt of Fell Head. The track, a Roman road, runs quite

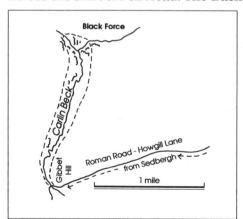

straight, leaving the
motorist in no doubt who
engineered it. Park on the
verge, called Gibbet Hill,
just before the track drops
steeply downhill to make
a hairpin bend over the
attractive bridge across
the Carlin Beck. Today,
after much rain in
preceding days, the water
surges beneath the arch
and flows on very fast

beneath the numerous trees that shade it for its short journey to join the River Lune.

Set off upstream on the south side of the beck. Close to the water the track is indistinct but you soon reach a better track and this continues for half a mile beside the dancing water. Bright green flushes with spearwort and forget-me-nots hide tiny feeder streams racing down to the Carlin. Meadow pipits, perhaps birds that will overwinter here, hurry across the slopes calling quietly as they fly. The track, following the course of the beck, swings to the right and into the shady, isolated seclusion of Carlin Gill. Before midday the sun is overhead and lovely shadows flit across the lonely slopes as clouds pass.

Occasionally the track leads down to grassy flats beside the chattering Carlin. Here delicate pink toadstools grow and a dipper feeds in the racing water. It utters a sharp single call as it flies upstream, then returns to feed in what must be a rewarding reach. Cross the pretty tributary whose upper waters can be seen cascading white-topped high above and then falling

Pink campion and foxgloves

104

over a series of rock steps in a haze of blown spray as the stream hurries down its grassy sunny gill.

Beyond this fall the sides of Carlin Gill becomes steeper and lined with ash and rowans, the latter clad in brightly coloured leaves and brilliant red berries. Look for the path which leads up the steep slope and continues into the narrowing gill. The path needs a cool head and a sure foot but there are rewards for those who manage it: they can pause along the path to view the Carlin tempestuously descend a steep drop in its bed, elegantly framed by trees; and look forward towards the distant Spout, a wide slash of foaming, white water where the Carlin makes its spectacular plunge into its gill.

Continue along the path until it reaches the foot of Black Force. The beck gathers its water on Fell Head, before descending into a hollow hidden in the upper recesses of this awesome canyon. Wide, white cascades descend below a rock lip through the precipitous gill where bilberry and heather, amazingly, maintain a hold and grow profusely. The sparkling, lace-like streamers continue their perpendicular fall, hitting rock ledge after rock ledge. The beck swirls on, moving to the left and to the right before racing excitedly past the path and eventually joining the Carlin in two spectacular streams. Here another dipper, with bright white bib and chestnut band, darts in and out of the spray gradually ascending the lower part of this exuberant fall.

Cross the Force and follow the tiny track that leads down to the side of the Carlin and to a place where the beck can be waded fairly easily. Return along the tracks. They looked easy from the other side of the beck but in fact require just as much care and concentration. One of the tracks leads over the scree, high above the companionable Carlin, and in time comes to a good high-level track across the fell. The afternoon sun is on your face and the fells are all around - all the previous scrambling along difficult tracks has been worthwhile.

The track leads into low-growing bronzed bracken over which hovers a kestrel. It dives several times into the dying plants, but each time ascends without prey. Above the grassy path a young buzzard also shows considerable interest in the bracken. It leans on the wind just above the plants, not moving its wings. It drops to the ground and stands for a moment. Then it rises and several times sails along the tops of the rusty-red fronds. As it flies away the sunshine catches its pale undersides.

The track leads downhill to the side of the beck. Continue beside it to the road. If the beck is in spate you will need to scramble and carefully negotiate boulders and eroded river banks.

Kestrel

Waterfall below the viaduct - Dent Head

23. Scow Force and Dent Head Viaduct, Dentdale

MR 774851, 776845,
1st waterfall - 50 yards, 2nd waterfall - ³/₄ mile

L EAVE SEDBERGH by a narrow leafy lane signposted Dent. In late October the thorn trees are laden with scarlet haws, the sides of the road are deep in fallen leaves and the views across the fells and up through the side valleys are unbelievably lovely. The lane leads into the village of Dent with its ancient houses gathered closely around the large, imposing church, and its narrow cobbled streets. Continue along the even narrower lane beyond Dent that leads into the quiet, isolated depths of Dentdale, keeping close to the River Dee. For six miles the river dances and cascades on its way to join the Rawthey and provides delightful accompaniment on the journey. Notice the milestones along the way.

Beyond milestone 10 park opposite Scow Cottage, where you can enjoy Scow Force and a restorative cup of coffee. Here, beside the road, the Dee surges over a wide, smooth rock bed beneath willows bright with lemon-coloured leaves. It then drops down a steep precipice in a foaming fall, the centre of which is stained with peat

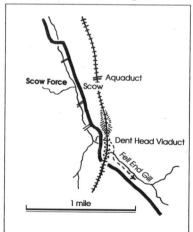

and framed on either side by lace-like cascades. Look for the ivy-leaved toadflax, with its purple and yellow flowers, that forms a tapestry on the wall at the side of the road. Here knapweed still flowers.

Drive on into the vale and park beneath the Dent Head Viaduct. The huge arches tower above, and overhead a tiny train journeys on to Dent Station. From this car park a smoking air shaft of the Bleamoor Tunnel can be seen on

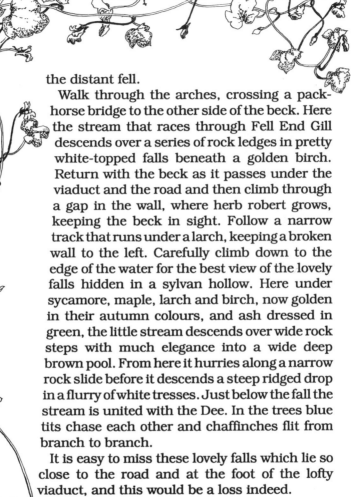

the distant fell.

Walk through the arches, crossing a pack-horse bridge to the other side of the beck. Here the stream that races through Fell End Gill descends over a series of rock ledges in pretty white-topped falls beneath a golden birch. Return with the beck as it passes under the viaduct and the road and then climb through a gap in the wall, where herb robert grows, keeping the beck in sight. Follow a narrow track that runs under a larch, keeping a broken wall to the left. Carefully climb down to the edge of the water for the best view of the lovely falls hidden in a sylvan hollow. Here under sycamore, maple, larch and birch, now golden in their autumn colours, and ash dressed in green, the little stream descends over wide rock steps with much elegance into a wide deep brown pool. From here it hurries along a narrow rock slide before it descends a steep ridged drop in a flurry of white tresses. Just below the fall the stream is united with the Dee. In the trees blue tits chase each other and chaffinches flit from branch to branch.

It is easy to miss these lovely falls which lie so close to the road and at the foot of the lofty viaduct, and this would be a loss indeed.

Ivy leaved toadflax

Hagg Beck

24. Hagg Beck, Horse Head Moor, Langstrothdale

MR 898779, 6 miles

B ETWEEN YOCKENTHWAITE in Langstrothdale and Halton Gill in Littondale lies Horse Head Moor - a vast expanse of high fell, the haunt of black grouse, meadow pipits and ravens. In late October a faint mist lies over the top removing the colour from the bleached and fading grass and the bronzed, dying bracken.

The two tiny hamlets, just a cluster of gracious limestone dwellings, are linked by a medieval pack-horse route, the Horse Head Pass, which ascends and then descends the steep sides of the sprawling moor. In the nineteenth century, Thomas Lindley, the parson of Halton Gill, held the village of Hubberholme, Langstrothdale, in his living. Each Sunday, whatever the weather, he felt it his duty to visit his second church, travelling the pass on horseback to minister to his parishioners until he was well into his old age. Today, long-distance runners cross it and walkers stroll

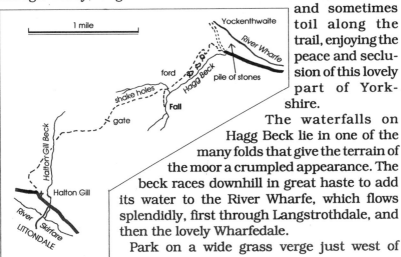

and sometimes toil along the trail, enjoying the peace and seclusion of this lovely part of Yorkshire.

The waterfalls on Hagg Beck lie in one of the many folds that give the terrain of the moor a crumpled appearance. The beck races downhill in great haste to add its water to the River Wharfe, which flows splendidly, first through Langstrothdale, and then the lovely Wharfedale.

Park on a wide grass verge just west of

111

Yockenthwaite. If you come from the direction of Hubberholme you find the verge on the left beyond the cattle-grid near the Pile of Stones marked on the O.S. Map. Take care to find an area of turf that is firm. The signpost for Halton Gill lies just beyond the cattle-grid but there is a wide grassy track swinging uphill from the verge and if you take this you can pick up the main route a few yards along.

The path is steep and ascends in a zig-zag before levelling out. To the left the wooded sides of the ravine which cradle Hagg Beck drop sharply and few trees are visible from the path, but here and there, where the gradient is less steep, you

Falls on Halton Gill Beck

can see rowan, ash and hawthorn. The rowans retain their multi-coloured leaves but the ash trees, still in green leaf, show no sign of autumn tints. Hawthorns, bereft of leaves, have attracted a crowd of mistle thrushes that flutter wildly through the branches feeding excitedly on a large crop of berries. A heron rises from the hidden beck and slowly wings its way towards the valley below.

Cross a ford over a small tributary which flows into the Hagg. To see the waterfalls, leave the main path and walk beside the stream. Beneath a rowan the stream leaps in a foaming jet before chattering on its way. Turn right and walk upstream beside the Hagg. The lovely beck drops through the austere slopes in a variety of falls. High up it descends in a long white plume before racing white-topped and angry over a series of semi-circular limestone steps. It then cascades in sparkling tresses as it negotiates another drop in its bed. It makes another pretty descent as it foams over steep, evenly spaced steps of rock. From here it dances on in more elegant cascades and falls, and is lost to sight as it descends towards Pile of Stones in the valley.

Return to the ford and continue uphill. The way is steep and muddy at times but take it slowly and look for the late buttercups and daisies flowering on either side. Look also for the shake holes on either side of the path and further away, towards the crown of the moor, the large peat hags. And be grateful that those who created the pack-horse trail knew where the firm ground was to be found.

The path leads to a gate in a drystone wall which marches across the top of the moor for many miles, stretching away in either direction. Beyond the gate a broad grassy track leads downhill - at last. Pause and look to the right to where Ingleborough lies veiled in thin drifts of mist, and then ahead to Pen-y-ghent, bathed in long streams of sunlight slanting through the clouds. Sunbeams race across the slopes as the clouds scud across the blue October sky.

The track swings away to the right, crossing several small streams, including Halton Gill Beck, hurrying down to the valley below. The good track, so easy to walk along, soon gives views into the lovely Littondale. The River Skirfare, turned to silver by the autumn sun, meanders placidly through walled pastures which slope gently upwards to the edge of the moors. Pass through several gates until the final one gives access to the road. Turn left and walk into the tiny settlement, which surely must have looked much the same a hundred years ago. Now the church and the school are private dwellings but a sense of timelessness remains.

Walk between the buildings and along the old track for a glimpse of the pretty falls on the Halton Gill Beck. Here blue tits, great tits, robins, wrens and hedge sparrows flit about the pastures, the water's edge and the walls. The chuckling beck passes beneath ash and through banks blue with germander speedwell and purple with herb robert before hurrying through the village and under the little bridge on its way to join the Skirfare. Find a quiet sunny corner in this tiny hamlet for your picnic before beginning the $2^{1}/_{2}$-mile return journey over the Horse Head Pass.

Clough Force
114

25. Clough Force between Garsdale & Grisedale

MR 783922, 4 miles

L ATE OCTOBER can bring days of cloud and mist, but neither can completely obscure the autumn tints of the trees and grassy slopes of the Dales. The banks of the River Clough, flowing over its uneven bed as it winds through Garsdale in a plethora of pretty falls, are lined with birches, ash, oak, willow, beech, hazel, hawthorn, rose and blackthorn. The trees, clad in a variety of reds and yellows, spread a cosy glow, making the walker forget the gentle drizzle and the wet ground beneath his boots.

Leave Sedbergh or Hawes by the A684 and park on the verge opposite the turn off for Garsdale Station. Here, where the footpath leaves the road, white deadnettle grows in profusion. Follow the indistinct footpath - signposted Grisedale and Flust - across the fell to the wall ahead where another signpost indicates

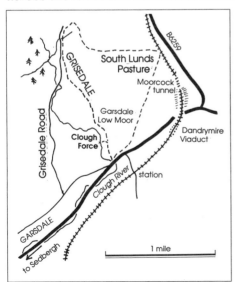

the way. Beyond the wall veer to the left aiming for a clump of sycamores. Walk down the slope to the right of the trees and Clough Force lies below.

The chocolate brown river, having flowed majestically between the bleak enfolding slopes, surges towards the force. It falls, gently at first, over a small thwarting ridge of gritstone before making its spectacular descent. The far side of the river foams white and streaked with

bronze for half its drop and
then the water, impeded
by a wide hidden ridge,
spurts into the air in a
series of horizontal foaming
spouts. The nearer side of
the river, unimpeded,
descends in an unbroken
fall, but a side flow of the
beck cuts into the bank
and then ricochets back,
causing a skirt of water to
fall across the uninter-
rupted fall.

*'a signpost shows
the way'*

On the fenced-off steep
bank leading to the river,
willows still retain some yellow leaves, and here ragwort flowers
and small rose trees carry a large crop of glossy red berries. This
lovely secluded hollow, where the waterfall descends, lies just off
the footpath, hidden by a grassy bluff. It is easy to miss but the
thunder of the raging water of the force is a sure guide.

Walk on along a narrow path beside the river and then climb the
slopes to a signposted gap in the wall. Beyond follow the footpath
as it moves diagonally across to the right towards Blake Mire (a
deserted farmhouse). After a night of rain the sphagnum and
polytrichum moss hold a large quantity of water. The various
species of sphagnum range in colour from green to yellowish white
and sometimes red; the other is a rich dark green and provides a
perfect contrast. Mat grass, growing alongside the moss, has now
turned to burnt sienna and partially camouflages a hen pheasant
feeding quietly just beyond the path.

Keep to the right of the farm and its three graceful ash trees and
follow the signpost directions just beyond the buildings, crossing
several walled pastures, all with well kept gap stiles. You come to
a farm track just beyond the dwellings called Rowantree. Cross
the track and follow the signpost directing the walker over a
pasture dotted with large clumps of rushes and on to Moor Rigg
and the Grisedale Road. Turn right and walk along the moorland
road, passing through East House Farm.

116

Continue through the gate beyond and follow a track that swings to the right onto the Grisedale Common. Walk along the track as it keeps parallel with the farm wall for a sixth of a mile and then veer away to the left, heading for the wall to the walker's left and leaving the well marked tractor trail. Beyond the wall follow the indistinct trail over the tops and then drop downhill over South Lunds Pasture to the cottages beside the Carlisle to Settle railway line. You have to cross a very muddy area to reach the stile that gives access to the footbridge over the track - take care here if you decide to climb the bridge because the wooden steps are excessively slippery. Do not cross the bridge but look for a small gated stile ahead. Beyond, walk diagonally to the right across the slopes to a broken wall; there is a good view from here of a small viaduct and the entrance to Moorcock Tunnel. Beyond the wall pick up a distinct path that leads onto Garsdale Low Moor.

Look for the ladder stile over the wall to the right of the path. Beyond this a wide muddy path continues, giving a good view of the trains passing over Dandrymire Viaduct. The path crosses the moor and through gaps in walls until at last it comes to the A684. Turn right and walk the few yards to your car.

Blake's mire

Thornton Force

26. The Waterfalls Walk, Ingleton

MR 693734 - the start of the walk, 4¹/4 miles

I N EARLY NOVEMBER the hedgerows and woodlands along the approach roads to Ingleton are ablaze with autumn tints. Once in the village follow the well placed signs that direct the walker to the waterfalls. The road drops down from Main Street crossing two bridges, one over the River Doe and the other over the Twiss. To the left is the magnificent viaduct beneath which these two rivers join to form the River Greta. To the right is the entrance to the large car park. The entrance ticket for the waterfall walk carries a small map showing the route.

The path out of the car park, bordered with ash, elm, hawthorn and field maple, the latter dressed in lemon leaves, leads to a kissing gate. Blue tits call cheerily as they hunt assiduously for insects. A jay flies, with a flash of its white rump and blue wing feathers, across the path to an oak on the other side. The River Twiss on its way to join the Doe, flows noisily over its boulder-strewn bed between alders and elms lining its banks.

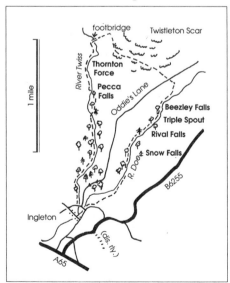

Once through the gate a reinforced path keeping close to the hurrying river leads through another kissing gate into the gorge of Creeping Steads. Several large yews cast a dense shade over the path. The ground is strewn with berries, scattered no doubt by the noisy flock of mistle

119

Pecca Falls

thrushes that regularly fly overhead. The high limestone sides of the gorge add to the shade but slanting shafts of sunlight still manage to penetrate the early mists of November. Alders, ash and oaks carry a blanket of moss in which polypody fern has taken root. Beneath the trees grow brambles covered with red leaves, herb robert flowers among golden-coloured, seeded grass and hart's tongue fern thrives in the lime-rich soil.

The path, climbing steadily above the deep brown water, leaves the gorge and rises into Swilla Glen. The lower slopes of the steep limestone cliffs are cloaked with hazel, sycamore, ash and elm where great tits meticulously search for prey. A wren sings loudly and cheerily from vegetation close to the water. Overhead wings a heron, head well back and legs stuck out behind.

Further up-stream, cross the roaring water by a footbridge and continue through hazel, elm and alder where self heal edges the track. A robin sings plaintively as if mourning the passing of summer. Walk on until the Pecca Falls lie ahead. Re-cross the river

Holly Bush Spout

121

by another footbridge at the bottom of the falls. From here you have a marvellous and awe-inspiring view of the raging water as it races, foaming and brown-flecked, down the steep slope above. Climb concrete steps to rise higher up the side of the impetuous river to where a huge buttress of rock spikes upwards and the water swirls on either side to fall in twin jets - the Pecca Twin Falls. Ferns and shrubs cover the rocky sides, splashed by the thundering water as it drops into a deep, foam-topped basin.

Continue climbing the steps until the highest fall is reached. This tosses spray over vegetation and walker alike and finally plunges into its own seething pool. The steps climb on past a railed area and close to a holly bush laden with scarlet berries that hangs over the topmost lip of the turbulent river before it rages downwards in a spectacular display. This is Holly Bush Spout. It has a dark cave at its foot.

Just beyond the topmost step is a small refreshment hut. In the

Beezley Falls

122

elms across the path a marsh tit hunts for insects. The path, occasionally paved with natural outcrops of green slate, leads out onto the open hillside, with the dark brown river flowing far below. Single ashes grow irregularly along the path and rowans, heavily laden with berries, flourish on the far bank of the Twiss.

Thornton Force is seen ahead. A wide flow of brown-streaked, foam-topped water falls downwards to a rock slide before it falls again, this time for forty feet into a surging pool. The vertical limestone layers just above the water of the pool contrast with the horizontal layering high above the fall. Yew, ash, oak, holly, rose and hawthorn clothe the slopes and the sides of the natural amphitheatre into which the force plunges before it cascades over boulders hindering its passageway. Over all rises a huge cloud of spray.

Climb the steps rising steeply up the slope high above the fall. Here the Twiss flows gently over broad, shallow ledges of rock. The steps continue and from these there is another delightful view of the lovely river. Then the path begins to climb once more and open country lies all around. On the far side of the ash-lined Twiss sturdy drystone walls criss-cross the pastures. Ahead stretch the extensive limestone outcrops of Kingsdale, its confining hills veiled in mist.

The path drops gently to the river and a footbridge leads to the other side. Climb the steps up the slope beyond the bridge, leaving the Twiss behind, and heading in the direction of the River Doe. Follow the path to a gate onto Twistleton Lane. Turn right along this wide, walled cart-track. Ahead in the bright sunshine lie pastures enclosed by walls stretching away into the far distance. Pass through two kissing gates and continue along the track as it winds below the limestone dotted slopes of Twistleton Scar End. Buttercups flower in the bleached grass bordering the track and scrubby hawthorn bushes lean over the drystone walls. A gate gives access to a metalled track. To the left is a fine view of Ingleborough, now sombre as rain clouds shadow its slopes.

Twenty yards along, just before Scar End Farm, look for a sign for Beezley Falls. The sign directs you over a stone-stepped stile beside a gate onto a muddy farm track. At the end of this track stone throughs by another gate lead to open pasture. A cement works lies to the far right, scarring the landscape and Ingleborough towers over all. Walk downhill to a kissing gate which leads onto Oddie's Lane, an old Roman road coming from Ingleton. Cross this, following the signpost directions. Walk down a track to Beezley Farm where daisies and buttercups flower along the grassy verge and a flock of rooks grub in a nearby pasture.

Pass through the outbuildings to a gate. Beyond look for a sign that points through oaks on the left to Beezley Falls. Here the River Doe descends in a wide surge of bronze-flecked water over thwarting boulders into a large brown-black basin between bare oaks and orange-leaved grass.

Follow the river downstream, on a path that is now softened by a deep carpet of rustling brown oak leaves. The path passes beside the raging water of the Triple Spout, just below Beezley Falls. Occasionally you will be splashed with spray as the wind catches and lifts small jets of water. Follow the path as it passes beneath oaks and below limestone cliffs to the Rival Falls where two exuberant foaming torrents descend. Both are bordered with larch and ferns, glorious in their yellow foliage. Oak too has saffron leaves and from these a mistle thrush calls harshly.

The walker uses concrete steps to climb and descend the steep slopes as the path finds the easiest route and at the same time gives splendid views of the raging beck negotiating the curves and varying levels of its bed.

The approach to the Baxenghyll Falls is most dramatic but withholds its most impressive vista until you stand on the viewing bridge. Three magnificent falls are seen far below, imprisoned by the sheer sides of the gorge. The beck foams, roars and boils as it is channelled into a narrow passageway. On every ledge in the perpendicular sides fern, ivy, bramble, herb robert, wood sorrel, hazel and wood sage grow where they can.

The path leads on among the trees, high above the river. Steps lead down to large, flat slabs of rock beside the water. A wren sings vibrantly and a flash of white reveals a tree creeper hurrying up the creviced trunk of an oak. The way, now alternately stepped and rough, leads to a small iron gate. Beyond the path continues until a gap in the trees gives an excellent view of the Snow Falls upstream and deep in a small gorge. A boulder at the top of the highest fall parts the water as it plummets downwards and then the Doe races through a pool to fall in another wall of white water.

Ash, oak, alder, birch and hazel cradle these lovely falls. Through the trees troop a mixed flock of coal and great tits.

Walk on down the leaf-strewn path to another bridge across the hurrying water. On the other side the path climbs upwards. It is bordered by hard fern, with both barren and fertile fronds untouched by autumn colours. It leads to an open area where the effects of earlier quarrying have now been softened by birch, ash, willow and hazel. Blue tits and chaffinches enjoy this sheltered sun-trap provided by the steep sides of the limestone cliffs.

The path continues through more oaks and then along the edge of pasture land separated by a drystone wall. Far below races the noisy Doe. Then the trees are left behind and ahead is a grand view of St. Mary's Church, now in November no longer obscured from view by the foliage of the trees about it. To the right, beyond the Doe, is another old quarry, its scars clothed in yellowing grass. Pass through a kissing gate and across a small tributary beck and follow the path to the road. This leads to Main Road and on to the two bridges over the two rivers and to the car park.

Rival Falls

125

Alum Pot
126

27. Alum Pot, Selside, Ribblesdale

MR 775756, 4 miles

E ARLY NOVEMBER, and the time for mists, short days and sometimes several hours of sunshine; on such a day a visit to the waterfall at Alum Pot, with the sun shining into the vast hole, can be most rewarding.

Drive along the B6255 until you are close to Batty Moss Viaduct. Here take the B6479 signposted Horton in Ribblesdale. Two and a half miles along look for a cart-track that leaves Selside Shaw Old Lane, as the road is named, just before a cluster of attractive dwellings and barns. Park on the side of the track or on one of the many verges. The surface is rutted and stony and much used by pot-holers for parking before setting off to explore.

Walk on up the cart-track, which is walled on both sides. Here a hedge sparrow repeats its constant high pitched song as it seeks for insects on top of the wall. Where the track swings away to the left take, instead, the stile beside a gate straight ahead. Beyond, a path moves out onto the open moor. Ahead, in the mist, lies

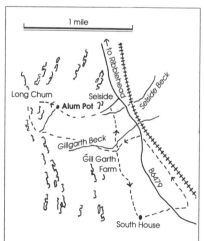

Simon Fell and Ingleborough. When the path suddenly ends walk on, heading towards a clump of trees. Alum Pot lies below these.

The huge chasm is surrounded by a wall but stiles give access to a path which stays close to the brink. Stand by the first ladder stile reached and look across the yawning gap to the lovely waterfalls beyond. At first the beck descend in white foam over a small drop in its bed and then it races on to fall, with a roar and in a mass of sparkling foam,

127

'leafless ash . . . festooned with large bunches of keys'

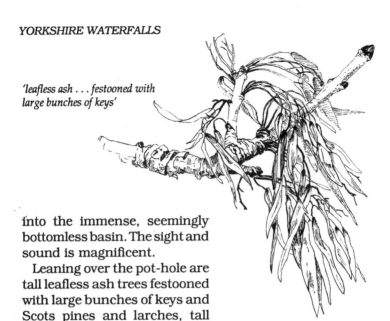

into the immense, seemingly bottomless basin. The sight and sound is magnificent.

Leaning over the pot-hole are tall leafless ash trees festooned with large bunches of keys and Scots pines and larches, tall and bent by the wind. By the waterfall, sheltered by rocky outcrops, grows a single, robust, splendid Scots pine. Beneath the trees and in the crevices flourish a myriad of ferns, with the long leaves of hart's tongue fern, a limestone lover, shining in the thin wintry sunshine that passes through the bare branches. Coal tits in the branches keep up an incessant short flock call. Walk to the left of the stile, nearer to the tumbling water. From here you can look across to where a misty haze hangs about the far side of the pot-hole. Two young elms lean over the depths, their yellow and orange leaves catching the mid-morning sun lightening the misty hollow.

Cross the beck and climb the immediate slopes. Then walk across the pastures to a ladder stile over the fell wall. Beyond lies a splendid limestone pavement. Here the twisted, tortured, brilliant white clints stretch away before you. In the grykes flowers herb robert among the rich green leaves of wood sorrel, wild thyme and more hart's tongue fern.

Walk across the clints and then follow an indistinct path that quickly comes to the edge of Long Churn, another pot-hole. All that the walker can see at first is a shallow dry river bed of smooth limestone. Then a fast flowing stream, visible for a few feet, drops

'gulls . . . glide across the sky'

noisily into a hole and is lost to sight. Here the pot-holers, first passing between walls of limestone, follow the water underground. A solitary rowan grows above the disappearing beck.

Strike away to the left across the moor, walking due south, keeping parallel with the wall that now lies to the left. After a third of a mile look for a gate in the wall which gives access to a grassy cart-track. Walk downhill along the track for half a mile and then, just before the wall at the back of Gill Garth Farm, turn right and walk across the pasture to a ladder stile. Overhead common gulls call as they glide across the sky, using the air currents.

Continue across pastures and two more stiles and then pass through a gap in the wall that lies to the left. Walk on through another gap in a wall and pick up a good track that leads to a gate into the yard of South House Farm. Walk down the farm road and cross the B6479 to a gate on the other side.

Walk straight ahead across the rough moorland until the wall on the far side comes into view. Look here for an indistinct footpath and follow it to the left (northwards) in the direction of Selside, crossing two stiles. Bear to the left to the far corner of the hilly pasture to a gate on to the roadside. Cross the road and walk back forty yards to a signposted footpath. High above flies a raven with strong measured flaps of its wings, uttering its deep bark as it goes.

Follow the direction of the signpost, passing through two gates. Turn right, this time in front of Gill Garth Farm, and continue to a gate on the left. Walk diagonally to the right across the pasture to a gate onto a walled track. At the end of this turn right into the stony cart-track, thus returning to the start of this delightful walk.

'a sparrow . . . seeks for insects'

Arten Gill Viaduct
131

28. Arten Gill Viaduct & Dockra Bridge, Dentdale

MR 776859, ¹/₂ mile; MR 756875, 1 mile

THE WINDSWEPT trees along the side of the road from Sedbergh to Dent, and from Dent onwards, are bereft of most of their leaves now that it is late November. Take the road out of Dent that keeps the River Dee to the south. Drive deeper into Dentdale and into the welcome peacefulness of this quiet valley. To reach the waterfalls below the viaduct at the foot of Arten Gill park in a large lay-by just before Stone House Bridge. Cross the bridge and follow the signpost directions for the gill. Overhead a heron, with head drawn back and long legs trailing, leisurely wings its way to the beck high on Blake Beck Hill. Blue tits chuckle cheerfully and great tits call from the branches of a magnificent beech in a garden beside the track. An equally magnificent sycamore stands close by, with some of its lower branches clad in pale lemon leaves.

For a short distance the track is bounded by scattered cottages and houses where chaffinches abound and a dunnock sits on a wall and sings its high-pitched song. Then, beyond a gate, the track swings steeply uphill to the magnificent viaduct that

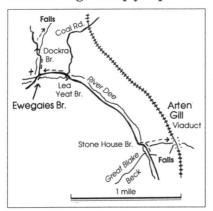

dominates the gill, making trees and houses alike seem small and insignificant. Look over the bordering wall to the waterfall that drops between two towering arches. As the Artengill Beck rages over the top lip of rock the wind catches the foaming water and funnels it up into the air. The beck then races down through the gill over a series of wide limestone steps, foaming and frothing, passing

leafless birch trees as it goes. It then descends in two white-topped falls, its glory undiminished by the viaduct towering above, before raging on to join the Dee above Stone House Bridge.

The viaduct, with its eleven arches, carries the railway over the gill and the track. Turn right beyond the enormous supports and with care walk to the edge of the steep grassy slope that runs down to the top of the falls. Here daisies and buttercups still flower unaffected in their lowly position by the fearsome wind that tangles with the water of the fall and buffets the viaduct. What difficult conditions the builders must have faced just over a century ago!

Return along the track to Stone House Bridge and walk along the road, upstream of the River Dee, to the end of the trees. These hang gracefully over the brown water hurrying over its broad, flat rock bed. Beyond the trees the Dee drops over steep ledges of rock in a pretty flurry

'with care walk to the edge'

133

of foam where a dipper busily seeks insect larvae and bobs and curtsies on a rock. Just below the fall the waters of Great Blake Beck having descended over similar rocky steps in curtains of white, joins the Dee.

Savour this delightful part of the river, then drive back a mile and cross Lea Yeat Bridge, parking on the side of the road close to the telephone box. Walk on along the road for a third of a mile to the turning on the right, just before the church of St. John the Evangelist. The church nestles among trees close to Cowgill Beck, the latter straddled by a bridge restored in 1702. Close by the bridge large sloes and lush blackberries burden bushes that have lost their leaves. A wide cart-track keeps close to the Cowgill, passing cottages on the right. In a verge below the wall, between beck and track, ragwort, Jack-by-the-hedge and herb robert flower. Towering overhead stands an enormous horse-chestnut with graceful curving branches. To the far right is Arten Gill Viaduct, complementing the line of the hills between which it is slung.

Cross Dockra Bridge and continue along the good track until it curves sharply to the left beyond an old barn. Away to the right beyond the pasture can be seen the waterfalls on the Cowgill. Enter the five-bar gate on the right into the pasture. Walk across to the edge of the beck and continue upstream. The Cowgill cascades over wide flat ledges under a larch aglow with golden needles and several ash trees, heavily laden with bunches of red-brown keys. It then plummets into a surging pool and hurries on towards Dockra Bridge and beyond to add its waters to the Dee.

'the track is bounded by scattered cottages'

Aysgill Force

135

29. Aysgill Force, Gayle and Mossdale Viaduct, Wensleydale

MR 865884, 2 miles; MR 826918, 1 mile

A FTER SEVERAL days of rain in the Yorkshire Dales you seem to find a waterfall round every corner; a delectable experience. And the falls are unobscured, in late December, by foliage; every dallying leaf has been ripped off by autumn gales and now these once lovely banners of many colours line the path, uniformly dull brown as they gradually return their goodness to the soil. The brilliant hued hips, the glowing berries of the hawthorn and the lush bounty of the elder have gone, too, devoured greedily by mistles, blackbirds, fieldfares and redwings. Tightly sealed buds alone remain on the skeletal trees, which are magnificent in their bared symmetry.

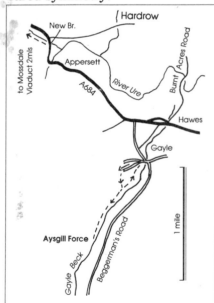

To visit the splendid Aysgill Force, leave Hawes by the signposted lane for Gayle which lies half a mile south from the small Yorkshire town. Turn left in the village and park in a wide paved area beyond the bridge over the River Gayle. Walk back over the bridge, pausing to look at the surging bracken-coloured water that flows with such magnificence over the wide limestone bed, stepped as it drops below the bridge.

Turn left immediately beyond the bridge and walk straight ahead among the old stone houses and barns that

136

'rooks, buffeted by the wind'

crowd the narrow roads leading out of Gayle. On the edge of the village, pass through a gap in the stone wall on the left, signposted Pennine Way. Walk straight ahead through a gap stile in the wall and continue ahead to another signpost. Follow the sign for the Force, passing through another gap in the wall on the right before walking across the field to another stile. Immediately beyond this bear to the left, looking for a series of restored steps that take the walker safely down a muddy, steepish slope to the riverside.

The path is bordered by coppiced hawthorn; coppiced once, perhaps, to provide denser shelter for sheep in the snow. The bushes are encrusted with lichen. Overhead fly several rooks, buffeted by the wind, but by the river the air remains still and the walker can hear the chuckle of blue tits and the pinking of chaffinches.

The way continues upstream through gaps and stiles and then rises uphill above the dancing water, where again the path has been pleasingly stepped. On the other side of the river rears a huge limestone scar with ash and Scots pine on its rim. Below, hart's tongue fern and lady fern have colonised faults in the limestone. A continuous carpet of alternate-leaved golden saxifrage, sprinkled with tiny golden flowers, extends from the foot of the scar to the water's edge. A ladder stile gives access to a path that leads along the edge of a gorge to the magnificent waterfall. At first the River Gayle drops quietly over several shallow steps in a series of cascades. Then it falls in one continuous wide sheet of water like a long white lace skirt into a deep dark pool, filling the canyon with its thundering and roaring. An ancient stone seat is placed at the right angle to enable the spectator to enjoy fully the beck's impetuosity.

Return to Gayle either by continuing along the path to the road and then turning left, or by taking the footpath above the riverside walk crossing pastures to reach the village.

Drive from Gayle to Hawes and then continue through Appersett. Beyond this hamlet the road slopes steeply downhill to the recently built Moss Bridge. Park in the large space on the right-hand side of the road beyond the bridge. Cross the road and walk down the gated road towards Mossdale Head. Continue walking towards Mossdale Viaduct, a four-arched bridge that used to carry a railway. Beneath the soaring arches the Mossdale Beck descends in glory. It rages over wide limestone steps that cause the water to boil and foam. After a smaller drop it descends again in a tempestuous fall before hurrying on to lose its energy in the River Ure.

Langstrothdale
139

30. River Wharfe, Langstrothdale

MR 891798 - 871803, 5 miles

PARK AT THE edge of the wide path, part of the Dales Way, at
Deepdale Bridge. Walk upstream along the bank of the Wharfe.
Here mallards sit on the grassy edge enjoying the thin November
sun and reluctantly take to the water as walkers pass too close.
Walk fifty yards along the path to where the surging, peat-stained
beck descends wide layers of limestone in a flurry of foam. Above
the water spread the bare grey twigs of ash trees that edge the
path. On the fell bracken turns to copper in the sun and the many
berries on the straggly hawthorn trees glow brilliantly red.

Continue past a plank footbridge. Look for the narrowing of the
limestone rocks that channel the water into tight confines beneath
the shadow of a tiny willow, still carrying all its leaves. A pair of
hedge sparrows nimbly hop along a wall and hunt for prey,
constantly repeating their high-pitched song. Another fifty yards
on and the Wharfe tumbles in pretty cascades under ash, berried
hawthorn and pussy willow with tiny grey downy buds. Here in a
flush, that adds a tiny flow of water to the main stream, large
patches of bright green-leaved saxifrage grow.

Walk on along the path to where limestone boulders divide the

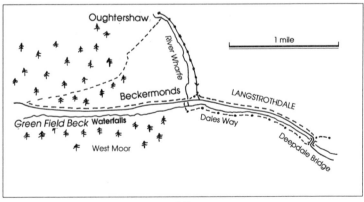

140

lively beck so that it drops in two foaming falls framed by leafless ash trees on either bank. Climb the ladder stile beside the falls and walk across the wide meadow that edges a sweeping curve in the graceful river. Here a pair of dippers - short-tailed, rotund birds - fly upstream to settle on a rock in mid-stream. Another bird settles on a nearby rock and is joined by one of the original pair. These two begin to bob up and down, displaying angrily, until the intruder leaves and heads back down the river.

Continue along the path to where the river makes another spectacular drop. Here the fall is wide and foaming, the water descends into a deep pool. In the shallows that cover the bed of limestone above the fall another pair of dippers walk into the swift flowing water seeking small larvae and the air is full of the shrill calls of these industrious birds and the sounds of tumbling water.

The Dales Way continues beside the beck past an ancient drystone wall until it comes to a meeting of waters where the Green Field Beck joins the Wharfe. The latter flows from Oughtershaw and passes beneath a handsomely proportioned bridge before gathering the water issuing from beyond Beckermonds.

The path ends by a narrow wooden bridge across the Green Field Beck. Cross the bridge - or use the stepping-stones if the flow of water permits. Beyond, walk up the grassy track between walls to a gate that gives access to a metalled and gated road. Turn left and follow

'pussy willow with tiny green downy buds'

the road as it passes through farm buildings and then out onto the open pastures, well stocked with sheep. Away to the left look for the lovely falls on the beck as it hurries through the valley to join the Wharfe. Beyond lies West Moor, planted with larch and fir - the latter, clad in dark green needles, providing the perfect foil for the soft yellow of the autumnal larch. Look, too, for the limestone rocks away to the right of the road, twisted and tortured into monstrous shapes.

A family of pheasants feed quietly by the fast flowing water and then, when disturbed, take to wing and, with a noisy whirr, fly to the safety of the plantation. A heron, too, when disturbed flies slowly upstream looking for a quieter place to feed. Continue along the road, passing through its several gates. Pause here and look back to where the sun streams across the slopes of Langstrothdale. Ahead the familiar mass of Ingleborough comes into view. On the right, a signposted gate indicates a track through the forest and then over the fields to Oughtershaw. If you decide to return this way turn right at the small settlement. Walk down the narrow moorland road and then along the dale to where you have parked your car. Or you may wish to return along the gated road, using either the Dales Way on the south side of the Wharfe or the road to Deepdale Bridge to return to your car.

'a family of pheasants feed quietly'
142

CICERONE GUIDES

Cicerone publish a wide range of reliable guides to walking and climbing in Europe

FRANCE
TOUR OF MONT BLANC
CHAMONIX MONT BLANC - A Walking Guide
TOUR OF THE OISANS: GR54
WALKING THE FRENCH ALPS: GR5
THE CORSICAN HIGH LEVEL ROUTE: GR20
THE WAY OF ST JAMES: GR65
THE PYRENEAN TRAIL: GR10
TOUR OF THE QUEYRAS
ROCK CLIMBS IN THE VERDON

FRANCE / SPAIN
WALKS AND CLIMBS IN THE PYRENEES
ROCK CLIMBS IN THE PYRENEES

SPAIN
WALKS & CLIMBS IN THE PICOS DE EUROPA
WALKING IN MALLORCA
BIRDWATCHING IN MALLORCA
COSTA BLANCA CLIMBS

FRANCE / SWITZERLAND
THE JURA - Walking the High Route and Winter Ski Traverses

SWITZERLAND
WALKS IN THE ENGADINE
THE VALAIS - A Walking Guide
THE ALPINE PASS ROUTE

GERMANY / AUSTRIA
THE KALKALPEN TRAVERSE
KLETTERSTEIG - Scrambles
WALKING IN THE BLACK FOREST
MOUNTAIN WALKING IN AUSTRIA
WALKING IN THE SALZKAMMERGUT
KING LUDWIG WAY

ITALY
ALTA VIA - High Level Walkis in the Dolomites
VIA FERRATA - Scrambles in the Dolomites
ITALIAN ROCK - Selected Rock Climbs in Northern Italy
CLASSIC CLIMBS IN THE DOLOMITES

OTHER AREAS
THE MOUNTAINS OF GREECE - A Walker's Guide
CRETE: Off the beaten track
Treks & Climbs in the mountains of RHUM & PETRA, JORDAN
THE ATLAS MOUNTAINS

GENERAL OUTDOOR BOOKS
LANDSCAPE PHOTOGRAPHY
FIRST AID FOR HILLWALKERS
MOUNTAIN WEATHER
MOUNTAINEERING LITERATURE
SKI THE NORDIC WAY
THE ADVENTURE ALTERNATIVE

CANOEING
SNOWDONIA WILD WATER, SEA & SURF
WILDWATER CANOEING
CANOEIST'S GUIDE TO THE NORTH EAST

CARTOON BOOKS
ON FOOT & FINGER
ON MORE FEET & FINGERS
LAUGHS ALONG THE PENNINE WAY

Also a full range of guidebooks to walking, scrambling, ice-climbing, rock climbing, and other adventurous pursuits in Britain and abroad

CICERONE GUIDES

Cicerone publish a wide range of reliable guides to walking and climbing in
Britain - and other general interest books

LAKE DISTRICT - General Books
LAKELAND VILLAGES
WORDSWORTH'S DUDDON REVISITED
THE REGATTA MEN
REFLECTIONS ON THE LAKES
OUR CUMBRIA
PETTIE
THE HIGH FELLS OF LAKELAND
CONISTON COPPER A History
LAKELAND - A taste to remember (Recipes)
THE LOST RESORT?
CHRONICLES OF MILNTHORPE
LOST LANCASHIRE

LAKE DISTRICT - Guide Books
CASTLES IN CUMBRIA
WESTMORLAND HERITAGE WALK
IN SEARCH OF WESTMORLAND
CONISTON COPPER MINES
SCRAMBLES IN THE LAKE DISTRICT
MORE SCRAMBLES IN THE LAKE DISTRICT
WINTER CLIMBS IN THE LAKE DISTRICT
WALKS IN SILVERDALE/ARNSIDE
BIRDS OF MORECAMBE BAY
THE EDEN WAY

NORTHERN ENGLAND (outside the Lakes
THE YORKSHIRE DALES A walker's guide
WALKING IN THE SOUTH PENNINES
LAUGHS ALONG THE PENNINE WAY
WALKS IN THE YORKSHIRE DALES (2 VOL)
WALKS TO YORKSHIRE WATERFALLS
NORTH YORK MOORS Walks
THE CLEVELAND WAY & MISSING LINK
DOUGLAS VALLEY WAY
THE RIBBLE WAY
WALKING NORTHERN RAILWAYS EAST
WALKING NORTHERN RAILWAYS WEST
HERITAGE TRAILS IN NW ENGLAND
BIRDWATCHING ON MERSEYSIDE
THE LANCASTER CANAL
FIELD EXCURSIONS IN NW ENGLAND
ROCK CLIMBS LANCASHIRE & NW
THE ISLE OF MAN COASTAL PATH

DERBYSHIRE & EAST MIDLANDS
WHITE PEAK WALKS - 2 Vols
HIGH PEAK WALKS
WHITE PEAK WAY
KINDER LOG
THE VIKING WAY
THE DEVIL'S MILL (Novel)
WHISTLING CLOUGH (Novel)
WALES & WEST MIDLANDS
THE RIDGES OF SNOWDONIA
HILLWALKING IN SNOWDONIA
ASCENT OF SNOWDON
WELSH WINTER CLIMBS
SNOWDONIA WHITE WATER SEA & SURF
SCRAMBLES IN SNOWDONIA
ROCK CLIMBS IN WEST MIDLANDS
THE SHROPSHIRE HILLS A Walker's Guide

SOUTH & SOUTH WEST ENGLAND
WALKS IN KENT
THE WEALDWAY & VANGUARD WAY
SOUTH DOWNS WAY & DOWNS LINK
COTSWOLD WAY
WALKING ON DARTMOOR
SOUTH WEST WAY - 2 Vol

SCOTLAND
SCRAMBLES IN LOCHABER
SCRAMBLES IN SKYE
THE ISLAND OF RHUM
CAIRNGORMS WINTER CLIMBS
WINTER CLIMBS BEN NEVIS & GLENCOE
SCOTTISH RAILWAY WALKS
TORRIDON A Walker's Guide
SKI TOURING IN SCOTLAND

THE MOUNTAINS OF ENGLAND & WALES
VOL 1 WALES
VOL 2 ENGLAND

*Also a full range of guidebooks
to walking, scrambling, ice-climbing,
rock climbing, and other adventurous
pursuits in Europe*

*Other guides are constantly being added to the Cicerone List.
Available from bookshops, outdoor equipment shops or direct (send for price list)
from CICERONE, 2 POLICE SQUARE, MILNTHORPE, CUMBRIA, LA7 7PY*